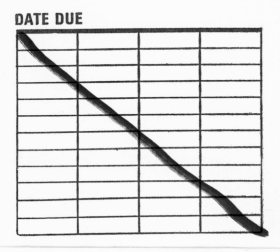

CIVIL LIBERTIES AND THE CONSTITUTION

Civil Liberties and the Constitution

Paul G. Kauper

GREENWOOD PRESS, PUBLISHERS
WESTPORT, CONNECTICUT

Library of Congress Cataloging in Publication Data

Kauper, Paul G
    Civil liberties and the Constitution.

    Reprint of the ed. published by the University of
Michigan Press, Ann Arbor.
    Includes index.
    1. Civil rights--United States. I. Title.
[KF4749.K37 1980]   342'.73'085   79-26222
ISBN 0-313-22223-1 lib. bdg.

Reprinted with the permission of University of Michigan
Press.

Reprinted in 1980 by Greenwood Press, Inc.
51 Riverside Avenue, Westport, CT 06880

Printed in the United States of America

10 9 8 7 6 5 4 3 2 1

PREFACE

In this book, I choose to deal with selected problems—describing critical areas in current constitutional development—that are matters of vital concern to every citizen. In particular, I have emphasized topics concerned with various aspects of the civil liberties protected by the Constitution. The choice of the specific subjects is due in part to the desirability of presenting for review and analysis recent major decisions by the United States Supreme Court—decisions that are important not only because of their intrinsic significance but also because they portray current trends and reveal the fluidity and movement that characterize the whole process of constitutional interpretation. A study of the decisions of the Supreme Court in recent decades makes clear that the larger part of constitutional litigation now turns on questions relating to protection of the freedoms secured by the Constitution, whether they be substantive or procedural in character. It is in the area of free speech, free press, freedom of religion, separation of church and state, and the equal protection of the laws that we presently find the fighting issues as far as constitutional interpretation of the substantive liberties is concerned. The aspects of freedom discussed in these lectures pertain to these issues.

The Supreme Court's decisions in the Sunday closing law cases and the controversy over proposals for federal aid to parochial as well as public schools highlight the contemporary significance of church-state problems and of the constitutional aspects of the separation principle—matters discussed in the first chapter. The important free press problems arising from obscenity legislation and movie censorship laws dealt with by the Court in recent cases furnish the theme of the second chapter. In the third chapter I survey at the outset the Court's recent decisions dealing with restrictive measures directed against Communists and contrast the decisions turning on the right of association and freedom from compulsory disclosure of membership lists. In view of the sharp cleavage within the Court in respect to this matter, I devote the latter part of this chapter to a consideration of the balance-of-interest technique, as opposed to the so-called absolutist approach, in the interpretation of the First Amendment. The last two chapters are directed to questions that relate to the nation's paramount problem, namely, the problem of making effective the constitutional guarantee of equal protection of the laws regardless of race or color. The fourth chapter deals essentially with the questions whether and under what circumstances the sanctioning by a state of discriminatory action by private persons and by private associations results in violation of the constitutional guarantee of equal protection. Consideration is given to the problem whether a state may enforce its trespass statute against persons who "sit-in" at a lunch counter in protest against racial discrimination. Discussion of these problems furnishes occasion for a survey of the decisions turning on the question of "state action." In the fifth and last chapter I have attempted an over-all survey of the tools and techniques available to the federal government in respect to the promotion and protection of civil liberties. Attention is centered on the political role of the federal judiciary in the interpretation and enforcement of constitutional guarantees as well as on the legislative competence of Congress to deal with these matters and on the executive function in these areas. The right to vote free from racial discrimination and the significance of recent Congressional legislation to safeguard this right receive consideration at this point.

In the presentation of these subjects I have in each case presented a general background designed to furnish a suitable frame of reference for appraising the significance of recent developments and their impact on specific problems. I have endeavored to keep the discussion practical, concrete, and informative, with emphasis on central issues, and without any attempt at exhaustive analysis of the problems.

This book is based on lectures which I delivered at the Special

Summer School for Lawyers held at the University of Michigan Law School in June, 1961. No substantial departure has been made from the text of the lectures as originally prepared and delivered. In documenting these lectures I have avoided extensive and exhaustive footnotes and have attempted to keep the footnote references to a minimum by citing only primary sources referred to in the text. In a few instances secondary sources have been cited where they seemed particularly desirable.

I acknowledge my indebtedness to the Law School, which sponsored the lectures, and to the lawyers whose favorable response lent encouragement to their publication with the hope of reaching a wider audience.

Paul G. Kauper

CONTENTS

I. CHURCH AND STATE: CO-OPERATIVE SEPARATISM   3

The Relevant Constitutional Limitations – Supreme Court's Interpretation of the Separation Principle – Critique of the Separation Principle – Government and Religious Education

II. OBSCENITY AND CENSORSHIP:
PROTECTING THE PUBLIC MORALS   52

Free Press and Constitutional Limitations – Basic Principles Established by Judicial Interpretation – Validity of and Limitations upon Obscenity Legislation – Censorship of Movies

III. FREEDOM OF ASSOCIATION AND FREEDOM FROM
DISCLOSURE: THE BALANCING OF INTERESTS   90

Five Recent Decisions by the Supreme Court – Freedom of Association and of Nondisclosure – Freedom of Nonassociation – Freedom of Political Association and the First Amendment – Judicial Techniques in Interpretation of the First Amendment – Absolutism versus the Balancing of Interests

IV. PRIVATE AND GOVERNMENTAL ACTIONS:
FLUID CONCEPTS   127

Fourteenth Amendment as a Restraint on Governmental Actions – General Considerations – The Kinds of Governmental Action Limited by the Equal Protection and Due Process Clauses – Legislative Enactments, Executive Acts, and Judicial Determination of Controversies Involving Property and Contract Rights – Application of the Fourteenth Amendment Limitations to Private Persons, Groups or Associations

V. CIVIL LIBERTIES: THE ROLE OF THE FEDERAL
GOVERNMENT   167

Constitutional Powers of Federal Government Respecting
Civil Liberties and Civil Rights – Kinds of Liberties and
Rights That May Be Asserted Against States and Individuals
– The Distinction Between Protected and Created Rights –
The Enforcement Powers and Functions of the Three
Branches of the Federal Government

NOTES   207

TABLE OF CASES   225

INDEX   229

CIVIL LIBERTIES AND THE CONSTITUTION

I. CHURCH AND STATE:
CO-OPERATIVE SEPARATISM

Nothing is better calculated to stimulate argument, arouse controversy, excite the emotions, and even produce intense visceral reactions than a discussion of church-state relations. Always a subject of lively interest, it has received added attention and emphasis in the recent months. Perhaps at no time in at least the modern era of American history have the questions of the proper relationship between religion and government been more thoroughly publicized and explored and the issues more widely debated than during the period beginning with the presidential campaign of 1960.

The nomination by the Democratic party of a Catholic for the presidency sparked the new public discussion of church-state relations and, more particularly, the question whether or not an adherent of the Catholic faith could properly discharge the functions of the President of the United States. Opposition to election of a Catholic to the presidency was based on the premise that the Catholic Church does not recognize the traditional American separation doctrine and, therefore, a Catholic president could not be expected to act in conformity with this doctrine. In response to these charges, Mr. Kennedy took a clear and unequivocal position in support of the separation of church and state.

Whether Mr. Kennedy's Catholic religion helped or hurt in the course of the campaign is one of those debatable matters on which judgment may be withheld. What is important is that Mr. Kennedy won the election and thereby became the first Catholic to win and occupy the nation's highest office. His election may be viewed as marking a decisive step in the history of religion in the United States. It effectively symbolized shifts in status of the nation's religious forces.

It is fair to say that from the time of the early settlements until the recent decades, Protestantism has been the dominant religious force in helping to shape the pattern of American life and the content of American culture. But the growth in size, power, and influence of the Catholic and Jewish minorities has pointed up a significant new pattern of American religious pluralism which marks the end of the so-called Protestant era in American history. This, in turn, has a vital bearing on all problems of church-state relations. The recognition that the Catholic and the Jewish groups along with the Protestant groups must all be recognized as standing in equal positions and that none has a preferred position either in determining governmental policy, or in choice of officers, or in molding the religious mores of the country has a significance far transcending the election of a Catholic as President. It became apparent some years ago that as the influence of the Catholic and Jewish constituencies increased, traditional Protestant assumptions would have to be discarded. Nowhere were these assumptions more clearly articulated and expressed than in the field of education. The public school system as it first developed and as it has continued in some parts of the country to this day was essentially a Protestant school system, and it is not surprising that despite the Protestant emphasis on separation of church and state, the reading of the King James version of the Bible as a devotional exercise was not uncommonly an accepted part of the public school program. And the idea that no public funds should go to support competing schools, notably parochial or religious schools, has revealed another distinctive aspect of Protestant thinking.

The current interest in church-state questions has been generated not only by the discussions of the religious issue in the course of the presidential campaign of 1960, but also by concrete legislative proposals that have a direct bearing on the problem. The President's proposal for federal aid to education,[1] whereby federal funds will be used to subsidize either capital expenditures or operating expenses, or both, of public schools throughout the nation, immediately provoked the question whether some federal aid should not be extended also to non-public schools including the parochial schools operated by church bodies. The Catholic hierarchy, supported by some other groups including a national organization of Orthodox Jews, is pushing a proposal that the federal government at least make low-rate interest loans available to nonpublic schools to assist in the construction of badly needed new and additional facilities.[2] The President has ventured the opinion that assistance of this kind to church-operated schools would be unconstitutional.[3] On the other hand, the President's aid-to-education program, while denying subsidies to nonpublic schools at the primary and secondary level, encompasses proposals for federal subsidies in the field of higher education, including loans or grants to church-related colleges for capital purposes, tuition grants to students attending these colleges, and further payments to these colleges, which raise similar constitutional issues.

Decisions by the Supreme Court during the past term add further interest to discussion of these problems. A Maryland law requiring that a person seeking an appointment as notary public take an oath declaring his belief in God has been held unconstitutional.[4] Much more significant, however, were the decisions dealing with the validity of Sunday closing laws.[5] The opinions in the cases, which will be discussed at some length later, furnish much interesting reading on the separation issue.

Enough has been said to indicate that the problems of church-state relations are with us in a very real and intimate way. A number of groups and organizations are devoting new study to these questions in order to clarify their position. While it might seem that the term "separation of church and state" solves all these questions, it has become clear to the thoughtful observer that the relationship between the political and the religious forces of the community, all operating within the same social structure, and often serving concurrent or overlapping purposes, and drawing upon the same basic human resources and personnel, is a matter too complex to be described by use of slogans or symbols, and that the problems attending this relationship are too difficult to be solved by doctrinaire propositions or absolutes.

The Relevant Constitutional Limitations

"Separation of church and state" is the symbolic language so often used as a beginning point of discussion. Actually, this precise language does not have much relevancy to the American scene. It is borrowed from European history and tradition where the problem could be identified in terms of a single church and of a single state or in later years of a single state and two churches, namely, Catholic and Protestant. To speak of separation of church and state in the United States invites some difficulty in the use of terms, first, because we have a plurality of states including the federal government and the individual states and, secondly, because we have a plurality of church bodies. Perhaps it would be more illuminating to identify the subject in terms of the problems arising out of the interrelationship of religious and political forces in the community. The term "state" denotes the politically organized community with its monopoly of coercive power. The church, on the other hand, is a voluntary association which must depend on noncoercive religious motivation and persuasion in making its impact upon the individual and the community.

The problems we are concerned with have a substantial legal significance since both the Constitution of the United States and the constitutions of the several states include provisions that deal with the church-state problem. The First Amendment to the Constitution provides that Congress shall make no law respecting an establishment of religion or prohibiting the free exercise thereof. Many of our state constitutions have provisions more explicit than this and designed, in many cases, to make clear that public property and public money shall not be used for religious or sectarian purposes or in aid of sectarian education. Moreover, the Supreme Court of the United States has said that the provisions of the First Amendment are made applicable to the states through the Fourteenth Amendment's Due Process Clause,[6] so that as a matter of federal constitutional restriction, and in addition to or apart from the limitations imposed by its own constitution, each state must observe the limitation that it can make no law respecting an establishment of religion or prohibiting the free exercise thereof.

In any discussion of the constitutional aspects of church-state relations, it will be useful at the outset to turn to general ideas developed by the Supreme Court in the interpretation of the First Amendment in order to appreciate the legal questions underlying current developments. The emphasis will necessarily be upon the First Amendment, both for the reason that some of the most significant current questions have to do with the limitations on the federal government and for the further reason, as already mentioned, that the Supreme Court has said that this limitation is made applicable to the states through the Fourteenth Amendment.[7] Indeed, we here have the curious situation that in order to find the meaning of the First Amendment as a restriction on Congress, we must look to recent decisions of the Court construing the Fourteenth Amendment, since in determining the limitations on the states under the Due Process Clause of the Fourteenth Amendment the Court has used the First Amendment as a controlling standard.

The First Amendment says nothing explicitly about separation of church and state. This term is not used in the federal constitution and, indeed, it is not used in American constitutions generally. This phrase is useful as a shorthand term for conveying a set of related ideas, but it is not a legal term, and certainly not a definitive constitutional term. What the First Amendment does say is that Congress shall make no law respecting an establishment of religion or prohibiting the free exercise thereof. Two different although related ideas are expressed in this opening clause of the First Amendment. Congress shall make no law respecting an establishment of religion, and Congress shall make no law prohibiting the free exercise of religion. Ordinarily, when people think of religious freedom they are thinking of the kind of freedom protected by this second part of the opening language of the First Amendment, namely, that Congress shall make no law prohibiting the free exercise of religion. Freedom to exercise one's religion is, indeed, a fundamental

right protected under the Constitution. It embraces freedom
of worship, freedom in the organization of religious associations, freedom in the propagation of the faith, freedom in
the distribution of religious literature, freedom in the enjoyment of public facilities dedicated to the dissemination and
propagation of ideas, freedom from discrimination on religious
grounds in the enjoyment of rights and privileges. This encompasses a wide field.[8]

The question may be raised whether the enjoyment of these
freedoms is dependent on the separation of church and state.
If, for instance, there is an established church, as in England,
is this incompatible with the free exercise of religion? Some
would say not and point to England as an example. The
Anglican church is the established Church of England. But
is there not complete freedom of religion in England? All
nonconformist and dissenting religious groups are free to
pursue their own ways. No one's faith is coerced. This is not
quite the case. The clergy and members of the Church of
England are really not free to exercise their own religion since
control of the Church is technically in the hands of Parlia-
ment. No established church subject to governmental control
or dependent upon governmental support is really completely
free. Moreover, members of independent churches are not
completely free to propagandize their beliefs in the market
place of ideas if they are competing with a religion enjoying
a preferred status established and supported by law. Nonestablishment as a rule requiring neutrality as between religions is then an important facet of the central concept of
religious freedom. On the other hand, if nonestablishment
means that government must be completely indifferent to
religion and that it can do nothing which aids religion in any

way, even though not preferential or discriminatory, the relationship of nonestablishment to the free exercise of religion becomes a more complicated matter. If the government without dictating or coercing belief on anyone's part recognizes the place of religion in the life of the community, and, without preferring one or more religious groups, accommodates its program and the use of its facilities to religious needs and supports activities in which the government and the churches have a concurrent interest and common concern, religious freedom is not placed in jeopardy. On the contrary, it may be argued that the government is thereby contributing to religious freedom and making it more meaningful. Some situations may arise when a choice must even be made between the nonestablishment principle as broadly conceived and the principle that the government may not discriminate on religious grounds.

It is evident then that the critical problems in respect to the separation of church and state turn on the interpretation given to the first phase of the opening clause of the First Amendment, namely, that Congress and, as interpreted, the states shall make no law respecting an establishment of religion.

As previously noted, the Constitution does not employ the term "separation of church and state," much less the terms "wall of separation" or "complete and permanent separation of church and state." These are all phrases that have been coined outside the constitutional language. The Supreme Court has said that the twin phrases of the First Amendment, proscribing laws respecting an establishment of religion or prohibiting the free exercise thereof, combine to require a separation of church and state.[9]

Supreme Court's Interpretation of the Separation Principle

We turn, then, to the interpretation given this language by the Supreme Court in recent years, and for this purpose we shall take account of key statements found in important cases. The first occurred in the course of the majority opinion in the well-known and now famous *Everson* case,[10] where the Court held constitutional a local school board's action in providing bus transportation at the expense of public tax funds for children attending parochial as well as public schools. This was the specific problem before the Court, and the majority found nothing unconstitutional about the school board's action. It is evident, therefore, that much that the Court said in that case about what either Congress or the states may not do to aid religion was gratuitous. The principal paragraph of Justice Black's much quoted dictum in this case reads as follows:

"The 'establishment of religion' clause of the First Amendment means at least this: neither a state nor the Federal Government can set up a church, neither can pass laws which aid one religion, aid all religions or prefer one religion over another. Neither can force or influence a person to go to or to remain away from church against his will or force him to profess a belief or disbelief in any religion. No persons can be punished for entertaining or professing religious beliefs or disbeliefs, for church attendance or non-attendance. No tax in any amount, large or small, can be levied to support any religious activities or institutions, whatever they may be called or whatever form they may adopt to teach or practice religion. Neither a state nor the federal government can, openly or secretly, participate in the affairs of any religious organizations or groups and *vice versa*. In the words of Jefferson, the clause against establishment of religion by law was intended to erect 'a wall of separation between church and state.' "[11]

It will be noted that the Court in this broad language, purporting to interpret the nonestablishment clause, included some ideas that clearly come under the free exercise of religion concept. What appears in this dictum as distinctively an interpretation of the nonestablishment idea is that the government cannot set up a church, pass laws which aid one religion, aid all religions, or prefer one religion over another, force or influence a person to go to church, force him to profess a belief in religion, punish him for disbelief or nonattendance at church, levy a tax to support any religious activities or institutions that teach or practice religion, or participate in the affairs of any religious organizations or groups. In short, nonestablishment means that the government can do nothing to aid religion or force religion on any person. In terms of the right of the individual, this means that a person enjoys a constitutional right to be free from any governmentally sanctioned religion and free from any imposition by way of taxes to support religion. Finally, it should be noted that Justice Black concludes this part of his opinion by referring to Jefferson's famous statement that the Constitution is intended to erect "a wall of separation between church and state."

That nonestablishment should mean the government may not sanction a particular religion or establishment or force religion on anyone is understandable. Such a construction promotes both the freedom of the believer and the freedom of the unbeliever, and both are entitled to constitutional protection. On this basis the Court has recently held invalid the provision of the Maryland Constitution requiring a declaration of belief in God as a condition of holding public office.[12] It is clear also that the conscience of individuals should not be coerced by forcing them to pay taxes in support of a religious establishment or religious activities. But the statement in Justice Black's dictum in *Everson* that government cannot aid all religions presented more difficulty. Did this mean that the government could under no circumstances do anything to recognize and encourage the worth of religious activities? If this is what was meant, then, was this intended by the language used in the First Amendment? Scholars disagree on this.[13] Moreover, such practices as tax exemptions for property used for religious purposes, commissioning of chaplains for the armed services, religious services in the nation's military schools, use of public property such as sidewalks and parks for religious purposes, exemptions of conscientious objectors from military service, tax deductibility of contributions for religious purposes, and the preferred treatment under the income tax laws for housing allowances for ministers have been long sanctioned in American history and cast doubt on the validity of this interpretation. Surely there is aid to religion in one way or another in all these practices. Moreover, as Justice Black recognized in his *Everson* dictum, no one questions the validity of giving churches the benefit of the usual governmental services such as police and fire protection and water service.

It is clear that either the Court was painting with too broad a brush in condemning all aid to religion or was using the term in a special way that needed further clarification. In the end did Justice Black say anything more than that the Constitution forbids the kind of aid which amounts to an establishment of religion? The difficulty in the "aid to religion" concept is manifest in the dissenting opinion in the *Everson* case. The four dissenting justices apparently accepted everything that Justice Black said about the meaning of nonestablishment, but felt that the majority had made a wrongful application of the idea since, in their opinion, the use of public monies to send children to parochial as well as to public schools was an aid to the teaching of religion, which according to the majority thesis was forbidden by the Constitution. This illustrates the problem of interpretation and suggests also that a proposal to use federal funds to grant some kind of assistance to parochial schools cannot be summarily disposed of by saying that it is constitutionally forbidden in view of the dictum in the *Everson* case. Indeed, if the actual holding in *Everson* means anything, it points in the opposite direction.

The decisions that immediately followed *Everson* dealt with the released time problem. In the *McCollum* case[14] the majority held invalid a released time arrangement whereby public school property was used for the teaching of religion by teachers supplied by the primary religious groups, but at the expense of one hour per week of school time. Participation in the program was voluntary, and children whose parents objected to participation were assigned other school activities during this period. The majority of the Court considered the released time program to be an unlawful involvement by the public school system in a program of religious education. As the majority saw it, the churches were using the schools as a means of recruiting students for religious education classes under circumstances that resulted in coercion of students to attend. But here again we have a dissenting view, this time by Mr. Justice Reed, who felt that the majority were running the separation argument into the ground. In support of this he pointed to many instances in American history where the state had taken a sympathetic view with respect to education for religious purposes.

Broadly interpreted, *McCollum* could have meant that the separation principle derived from the nonestablishment limitation requires the state to be completely indifferent to religion and to the interest of parents in religious education. This is the only actual decision by the Supreme Court where the holding can be said to rest on a broad theory of separation of church and state. Actually, the case could easily be interpreted more narrowly to mean that the state may not make itself a party to any scheme whereby religious education is forced on children in the public schools. A broad interpretation of the case was repudiated by the later decision in the *Zorach* case,[15] where the Court sharply limited *McCollum* by holding that a program of released time for religious education of children in the public schools was constitutional provided that classes were not conducted on the school premises. For all practical purposes a majority of the Court had now swung around to the views expressed by Justice Reed in dissent in the *McCollum* case. This becomes evident when we look more closely at Justice Douglas' majority opinion and also at the opinions written for the four dissenting justices who argued strenuously that the distinction between this case and the *McCollum* case was insubstantial and even trivial and did not warrant a difference in result. The dissenters appear to be right in saying that there was no substantial distinction between the two cases. What is far more important was Justice Douglas' opinion in *Zorach*. Speaking for a majority of the Court he sharply limited the language previously used in the *Everson* case. Indeed, as *Zorach* is a later case, it is surprising that the *Everson* opinion is quoted in much of the current discussion of church-state problems in their constitutional aspects as though it were the only word on the subject. In the course of his opinion Mr. Justice Douglas said:

"There is much talk of separation of church and state in the history of the Bill of Rights and in the decisions clustering around the First Amendment . . . [here citing the *Everson* and *McCollum* cases]. There cannot be the slightest doubt that the First Amendment reflects the philosophy that church and state should be separated. And so far as interference with the free exercise of religion and establishment of religion are concerned, the separation must be complete and unequivocal. The First Amendment within the scope of its coverage permits no exception; the prohibition is absolute. The First Amendment, however, does not say that in every and all respects there shall be a separation of church and state. Rather it studiously defines the manner, the specific ways, in which there shall be no concert, no union or dependency of one on the other. That is the common sense of the matter. Otherwise the state and religion would be aliens to each other—hostile, suspicious, and even unfriendly. Churches could not be required to pay even property taxes and municipalities would not be permitted to render police or fire protection to religious groups. Policemen who helped parishioners into their places of worship would violate the Constitution. . . .

"We are a religious people whose institutions presuppose a Supreme Being. We guarantee the freedoms to worship as one chooses. We make room for as wide a variety of beliefs and creeds as the spiritual needs of man deem necessary. We sponsor an attitude on the part of government that shows no partiality to any one group and that lets each flourish according to the zeal of its adherents and the appeal of its dogma. When the state encourages religious instruction or cooperates with religious authorities by adjusting the schedule of public events to sectarian needs, it follows the best of our traditions. For it then respects the religious nature of our people and accommodates the public service to their spiritual needs. To hold that it may not would be to find in the Constitution a requirement that the government show a callous indifference to religious groups. That would be preferring those who believe in no religion over those who do believe. The government may not finance religious groups nor undertake religious instruction nor blend secular and sectarian education nor use secular institutions to force one or some religion on any person. But we find no constitutional requirement which makes it necessary for government to be hostile to religion and throw its weight against efforts to widen the effective scope of religious influence. The government must be neutral when it comes to competition between sects. It may not thrust any sect at any person. It may not make a religious observance compulsory. It may not coerce anyone to attend church, to observe a religious holiday, or to take religious instruction. But it can close its doors or suspend its operations as to those who want to retire to their religious sanctuary for worship or instruction. No more than that is undertaken here.

"This program may be unwise and improvident from an educational or a community viewpoint. That appeal is made to us on the theory, previously advanced, that each case must be decided on the basis of 'our own prepossessions.' . . . Our individual preferences, however, are not the constitutional standard. The constitutional standard is the separation of Church and State. The problem, like many problems in constitutional law, is one of degree. . . ."[16]

Justice Douglas' opinion for the majority in the *Zorach* case is quoted at length since it reflects a basic difference in approach. To be sure, it overlaps in large part what was said in *Everson*. The government may not finance religious groups, must be neutral between sects, cannot undertake religious instruction or force religion, religious instruction, or religious observance on anyone. There are notable points of difference, however, and these become crucial and central in any discussion of the problem. First of all the *Zorach* opinion recognizes that the First Amendment itself says nothing about the separation of church and state. Separation is not in itself a starting point in constitutional thinking. It follows and is required only to the extent that it flows from the clauses relating to nonestablishment and the free exercise of religion. The First Amendment then, according to *Zorach*, does not ordain a complete and absolute separation of church and state in every respect. Implicitly, the Court in *Zorach* repudiates the notion that the First Amendment establishes a wall of separation between church and state, for the wall terminology and imagery are based upon a notion of absolute and complete separation. Moreover, in *Zorach* the Court emphasized the idea that the legislative body of a state may take into account the religious interests of its citizens and adapt its legislative program to that end at least so far as accommodation of public facilities and services are concerned. Here, in other words, is a disclaimer of the idea that the state must be completely neutral as between religion and nonreligion. At least so far as the First Amendment is concerned, the Court says that the legislature may take account of the religious interests of its people in its legislative program so long as it does not act with coercive effect upon dissenters and nonbelievers and no preference is given to any one religious group. In short, the government is not required to act as though religion and religious institutions did not exist. Indeed, it may go further and find that they perform a useful and desirable function in the social community, even a public purpose, and that within the limits imposed by the Constitution their activities may be encouraged and favored by the state. Finally, it is significant that the Court said in the *Zorach* case that the problem of separation of church and state, like many problems in constitutional law, is one of degree. This may be the most significant statement in the whole case. The problems in this area cannot be solved by resort to doctrinaire absolutes, verbal formulae, or metaphors. As in all constitutional adjudication, the Court must look at these problems in terms of the competing interests at stake and, therefore, take a critical look at both what the state is trying to do and what the fundamental purposes served by the constitutional restrictions are.

Recent extended expressions of opinion in this important area are found in the Court's four decisions dealing with the validity of Sunday closing laws, and any discussion of the problems in this area must take these decisions and the several opinions into account. Indeed, the whole area of church-state relations and the basic meaning of the First Amendment are subjected to intensive review.

The basic constitutional problems presented in the four cases consolidated for hearing before the Court can be simply stated:

1. Is a state or local law, which states a general rule prohibiting work or business on Sundays, unconstitutional because it, in effect, is an attempt to establish to some extent the Christian religion as the religion of the community?

2. Even if such a law is not generally invalid on an establishment theory, must it as a constitutional matter exempt from its prohibition of Sunday work persons who because of religious convictions observe a day other than Sunday as a day of rest?

The majority of the Court found these Sunday closing statutes to be constitutional, both in their general application

and in their application to persons who for religious reasons observe another day of the week as a day of rest, as in the case of Orthodox Jews who abstain from business activities on the Sabbath.[17] The chief opinions were written by Chief Justice Warren and were concurred in by Justices Black, Clark, and Whittaker. A long concurring opinion was written by Justice Frankfurter joined by Justice Harlan. Justices Brennan and Stewart concurred in the view that Sunday closing laws are not generally invalid as an attempt to establish the Christian religion, but dissented from the majority's holding on the second question, since in their opinion it is a violation of religious liberty to force a Sunday closing on a person who already for religious reasons observes a different closing day. Justice Douglas dissented both on the ground that Sunday closing laws are unconstitutional generally as an attempt to establish the Christian religion and on the further ground that they violate the religious freedom of persons who observe a different day of rest.

As already noted, these cases raised issues under both the nonestablishment and the free exercise clauses. The argument in respect to establishment is easily seen, namely, that Sunday closing laws rest on the Christian conception of Sunday as a day of worship and rest, and that, therefore, these laws sanction the Christian religion as the official religion of the community. Admittedly, Sunday closing laws have their genesis in religious considerations. Eight members of the Court, however, are satisfied that the Sunday closing laws at issue in the cases before them, whatever the motivation behind their original enactment, are now justified on secular grounds as an exercise of the state's police power to promote the public health and welfare by establishing one day of the week as a day of rest, repose, relaxation, and family visiting. In short, the state has established a secular holiday for reasons appropriate to the state's police power, and the validity of its action is not impaired by the consideration that the day of the week chosen corresponds with the day observed for religious reasons by a majority group in the community. Once it is conceded that the Sunday closing laws rest on adequate nonreligious grounds, then, according to the majority, it is no violation of religious freedom to compel observance of the law by those persons who because of their religion, whether Jews, Seventh Day Adventists, or others, feel compelled to observe a different day of the week as a day of rest and thereby must make a choice between their religion and the economic disadvantage of having to observe two days of rest each week. On this point the majority relied on the well-established doctrine, supported by the cases, that the practice of religion is subject to reasonable exercise of the police power. Polygamy may be prohibited even though sanctioned by religion, public health measures take precedence over religious scruples against medical treatment, and the public interest may require a person to serve in the country's armed forces even though he is a conscientious objector. Citing the practical enforcement problems that would otherwise arise and the difficulties involved in use of a religious test, the Court concluded that the legislature was not acting unreasonably in denying exemptions from the Sunday closing law to persons whose religion required observance of a different day of rest.

On the surface of the matter and by reference to the history of Sunday closing laws one is tempted to support Justice Douglas' view in dissent that no amount of rationalization can serve to disguise the religious motivation behind these laws, but the lengthy opinions by Chief Justice Warren and Justice Frankfurter, together with the extended documentation, do lend impressive support to the idea of evolution and change in the motivation underlying Sunday laws and to the thesis that for many Americans Sunday is a thoroughly enjoyable day of rest and relaxation quite unrelated to the matter of religious observance. The transformation of Sunday from a religious into a civil holiday is an interesting symbol of the secularization of American society. Religious forms are appropriated for secular purposes.

What contribution do the Sunday closing law cases make to the interpretation of the nonestablishment idea? The cases do not really turn on any new interpretation of establishment, since it was recognized by all nine justices that Sunday closing laws would have to be condemned as an attempt to establish religion if they could be justified only by religious considerations. Reduced to capsule form, the holding in these cases is that governmental action serving a valid public purpose by reference to civil and secular considerations does not become invalid because it operates simultaneously to promote religious interests, either generally or of a particular group. So stated, the holding is parallel to that of the *Everson* case—spending public money to send children by bus to parochial schools serves a valid secular purpose even though it also advances and helps a program of religious education.

Although Chief Justice Warren's opinion[18] discusses the general theory and interpretation of the First Amendment at some length, in the end it relies chiefly on *Everson* as an exposition of the nonestablishment language. Justice Frankfurter's separate opinion is more instructive in this respect. He makes the principal point that the nonestablishment idea forbids governmental action which is directed toward the primary end of affirming or promoting religious doctrine. His opinion at this point is worth quoting at length:

"Of course, the immediate object of the First Amendment's prohibition was the established church as it had been known in England and in most of the Colonies. But with foresight those who drafted and adopted the words: 'Congress shall make no law respecting an establishment of religion,' did not limit the constitutional proscription to any particular, dated form of state-supported theological venture. The Establishment Clause withdrew from the sphere of legitimate legislative concern and competence a specific, but comprehensive, area of human conduct: man's belief or disbelief in the verity of some transcendental idea and man's expression in action of that belief or disbelief. Congress may not make these matters, as such, the subject of legislation nor, now, may any legislature in this country. Neither the National Government nor, under the Due Process Clause of the Fourteenth Amendment, a State may by any device support belief or the expression of belief for its own sake whether from conviction of the truth of that belief, or from conviction that by the propagation of that belief the civil welfare of the state is served, or because a majority of its citizens holding that belief are offended when all do not hold it. . . .

"To ask what interest, what objective legislation serves, of course, is not to psychoanalyze its legislators, but to examine the necessary effects of what they have enacted. If the primary end achieved by a form of regulation is the affirmation or promotion of religious doctrine—primary in the sense that all secular ends which it purportedly serves are derivative from, not wholly independent of, the advancement of religion—the regulation is beyond the power of the state. This was the case in *McCollum*. Or if a statute furthers both secular and religious ends by means unnecessary to the effectuation of the secular ends alone—where the same secular ends could equally be attained by means which do not have consequences for promotion of religion—the statute cannot stand. A state may not endow a church although that church might inculcate in its parishioners moral concepts deemed to make them better citizens, because the very *raison d'être* of a church, as opposed to any other school of civilly serviceable morals, is the predication of religious doctrine. However, inasmuch as individuals are free, if they will, to build their own churches and worship in them, the State may guard its people's safety by extending fire and police protection to the churches so built. It was on the reasoning that parents are also at liberty to send their children to parochial schools which meet the reasonable educational standards of the State, *Pierce* v. *Society of Sisters*, 268 U.S. 510, that this Court held in the *Everson* case that expenditure of public funds to assure that children attending every kind of school enjoy the relative security of busses, rather than being left to walk or hitchhike, is not an unconstitutional 'establishment,' even though such an expenditure may cause some children to go to parochial schools who would not otherwise have gone. The close division of the Court in *Everson* serves to show what nice questions are involved in applying to particular governmental action the proposition, undeniable in the abstract, that not every regulation, some of whose practical effects may facilitate the observance of a religion by its adherents, affronts the requirement of church-state separation."[19]

Although Justice Frankfurter's opinion serves a useful purpose in its analysis of the problem and with its emphasis on the "primary end" served by a regulation, the test proposed still requires a large measure of judicial weighing and judgment. Moreover, his statement does not purport to explain or harmonize all the earlier cases. The *McCollum* case may very properly be cited to support the proposition that the state may not enact a form of regulation which has as its primary end the promotion of religious doctrine. But Justice Frankfurter says nothing about *Zorach*, and the question may indeed be raised whether *Zorach* can be fitted into his analysis.

The weakness, if not futility, of attempts to state general propositions as controlling tests for these cases is further illustrated by Justice Douglas' dissenting opinion. The point of emphasis in his long and interesting opinion is captured in the following sentence:

"There is an 'establishment' of religion in the constitutional sense if any practice of any religious group has the sanction of law behind it."[20]

On the surface this sounds like a sensible and viable test. But, again, it may be questioned whether it states an accurate proposition. If a law prohibiting polygamy exempts those who practice plural marriage as a matter of religious conviction, if a law regulating the slaughtering and inspection of meat exempts from its requirements meat slaughtered and inspected in accordance with religious practices, if a public health measure exempts persons who are opposed to medical treatment on religious grounds, and if, indeed, a Sunday closing law grants an exemption to persons who observe a different rest day on religious grounds, can it not be said in each of these instances that the state is placing the sanction of law behind the practice of a religious group. Yet no one seriously supposes that any one of these exemptions would be held unconstitutional. On the contrary, they would be appropriately regarded as a legislative recognition and implementation of religious freedom.

Critique of the Separation Principle

In the light of these expressions of opinion and the holdings by the Court, what can be said about the meaning of nonestablishment and what is its relevancy to today's most urgent problems in this area?

In any critical examination of this general problem of church-state relations and more particularly of the nonestablishment limitation, it is useful to start with the elementary idea that the state and the church serve basically different functions and objectives. It is the state's business to operate the politically organized society and serve the community's civil needs. The business of the church is to minister to man's spiritual needs and to carry on activities appropriate to a sense of religious concern. It is not the business of the state to operate a church or to engage in the propagation of religious ideas. On the other hand, it is not the function of the churches to exercise the coercive authority of the politically organized community. This separation of function has its roots not simply in some theoretical conception of a convenient division of labor but is grounded more profoundly on the theory that the cause of human freedom is best served when religion and its institutions are grounded in voluntarism and not dependent upon political force.

The really important questions we face today, however, do not arise from any threat of formal confusion of functions or any attempt at formal institutional blending of the separate functions of the church and state. Rather they have to do with the practical problems of interrelationship involving questions of the recognition of the function of each and of the contribution that each makes to the total scheme of things.

Even though a separateness of function is recognized in

regard to the primary purposes of politically organized society and religious institutions, it is clear that this abstract idea must be given practical meaning in the context of a social community where both the secular and religious societies draw on the same human resources. This is what introduces the perplexing aspects of our problem. We may speak of a duality of citizenship—an allegiance to both the secular and the spiritual realms. Or, in Luther's terms, we have the two kingdoms: the kingdom of the sword and the kingdom of the spirit. Yet they must necessarily operate within the same community. From this it follows that each must respect the other, and, indeed, each is dependent upon the other.

The state has a complete monopoly of coercive power with the result that the church is necessarily dependent upon the state for the maintenance of the elementary conditions of peace and order essential to the enjoyment of religious freedom and to the discharge of the church's functions, whether it be the maintenance of a house of worship, propagation of the faith, teaching the young, or ministering to the sick and needy. It is an idea well accepted in Christian theology and doctrine that the state itself occupies an important role in God's created order and that its primary function in punishing the wrongdoer and preserving the peace of the community is to make possible the conditions that will advance the kingdom of the spirit. The church as the community of believers, therefore, respects the state and looks to the state for protection of the peace of the community, for protection of its property, and for enjoyment of the public services rendered by the state. Already at this point it becomes evident that there is an interdependence which is not accurately portrayed by the wall of separation metaphor. The church is dependent upon the state in a very real way in order to maintain its functions. For this

reason the church deems it appropriate that its members support the state, pay taxes, vote, and serve as magistrates and
civil servants despite the radical views of a small group within
the Christian communion who, in order to carry separation to
a maximum, have divorced themselves from the political life
of the community. It is appropriately the function of the state
to provide police and fire protection and to give churches the
benefit of the same services provided to other organizations
and to individuals whether it be in the furnishing of utility
service or whatever service the politically organized community
renders. Obviously, the state in giving the religious community
the benefit of these services is extending aid to religion in a very
real sense. To suggest that this is distinguishable because this
is not aid to religion as such is simply to use words to avoid
the critical problem. When government makes its facilities
available to protect organized religious groups and to make
possible the system in which religion can flourish, it is giving
the most important aid that a state can give to any group with
respect to the performance of its functions. It is aid to religion
but not the kind of aid forbidden by the Constitution. It is
a benefit shared by the church with all the community, and
the state in extending this benefit is not thereby using its
power to promote or sanction religious belief.

As the church is dependent on the state and depends for
its effective functioning and even survival on valuable services
furnished by the state, so, in turn, the politically organized
community expects to be served by the religious community.
The tradition developed in English legal history that the
Chancellor was the keeper of the King's conscience. This term
epitomized the idea that the King counted on conceptions of
equity developed by this ecclesiastical officer to liberalize the
Common Law and to infuse it with moral conceptions of a

basic religious orientation. This is simply another manifestation
of the idea that the churches in the discharge of their separate
functions—cultivating the spiritual lives of their parishioners
and developing moral and ethical ideas founded on religious
insight and motivation—make an important contribution to
the politically organized community. The state in formulating
policy and in fashioning the law must depend upon the moral
sense and values of the community. It makes little difference
whether we recognize the church's contribution to the legal
order and to the conception of public policy in terms of a
body of moral or natural law which serves as a guide or norm
for the framing of positive law, or identify this contribution
to the civic order both through the impact of religiously motivated citizens and public officers and the discharge by the
church of a prophetic function in speaking of matters of
public concern. In regard to such matters as disarmament,
the use of nuclear weapons as war weapons, birth control,
distribution of surplus foods to needy peoples, immigration
policy, aid to education, aid for the aged, the churches do
have a real, vital interest. These are matters of both religious
and civic concern.

There are some who suggest that separation of church and
state means that religion and politics must be kept separate.
If by this is meant that the church, in deference to the separation idea, may minister only to the spiritual needs of its members and not exercise a prophetic function in speaking to the
problems of our day, then we have a gross misconception of the
separation principle. Indeed, a higher principle arises here in
terms of religious freedom on the part of any person or group
to express ideas that have religious significance and which
are relevant also to current social, economic, and political
problems. Criticism is often made of the Roman Catholic

Church that it attempts to influence legislative policy in such matters, for instance, as birth control, sterilization, euthanasia, and obscenity in literature and the movies. On this matter it should be clear, first of all, that insofar as this is a separation problem it is not a constitutional problem, since it is part of the freedom of churches to propagandize and to use their efforts to influence legislative policy. The Constitution does prohibit giving to any church a formal place in the legislative process. But it does not prohibit the churches or their members from giving their opinions on matters of political concern or speaking in support of legislative proposals. This, indeed, is part of their function as religious bodies. The idea that a man's religion is irrelevant to his conduct as a citizen or as a public officer states a low view of religion and a sterile concept of the place of religion in influencing a man's conduct, attitudes, and motivations.

We may take as an illustrative case the problem of birth control. According to the doctrine of the Catholic Church, the use of means of artificial birth control presents a moral problem. Is it appropriate then for the church to advocate legislation designed to reflect the church's views on the subject, and in turn is legislation on this subject invalid as an establishment of religion? Legislation in regard to moral matters has been common throughout our history. Indeed, religious and moral grounds may be cited to support a large body of our criminal laws. For many, murder is a crime because it violates religious commandments. If a dominant segment of a community wishes to translate a moral idea into a law, this is nothing new nor does it violate any concept of separation of church and state in the constitutional sense. A dominant religious group may be ill-advised to do this and thereby impose its will upon others who do not accept, although this is usually true of the exercise of the police power. In the end, these questions must be discussed and answered in the course of the usual political and legislative processes. Although the Catholic Church has been singled out for the purpose of illustrating the question involved when a church presses for laws that reflect the church's views on moral questions, this situation is by no means peculiar to this church. President Grant reportedly said that there were three political parties in this country—the Republicans, the Democrats, and the Methodists.[21] At present, many church groups are identified with efforts to secure civil rights legislation. Obviously, the separation idea does not preclude this. On the contrary, any sensible, mature, and sophisticated understanding of the relationship between the church and the state must take account of these common areas of concern and recognize that ideas and values of religious significance may appropriately be translated into or identified with conceptions of public policy and interest in the proper reach of governmental power.

There is, of course, an end point reached in the use of the legislative power to promote views, programs, or practices that have a religious significance. A distinction must be made between legislation which finds support in considerations of public interest, even though also identifiable with religious views and practices, and legislation designed to force a religious view or practice upon the community. The latter must be condemned as an unconstitutional establishment of religion. Obviously, a statute requiring every person to attend church on Sunday or to make a contribution in support of churches would be invalid. This is the use of the state's power to promote a strictly religious objective, and no secular or civil considerations can justify such legislation. On the other hand, the Supreme Court, in the recent cases discussed earlier, has held that Sunday closing laws are a valid exercise of the state's police power since they rest on adequate secular or civil considerations even though they may also serve the concurrent purpose of promoting observance of the Christian religion.

Let us return for a moment to birth control laws. The Supreme Court at its last term handed down its decision dealing with the validity of the Connecticut statute prohibiting the use and sale of artificial birth control devices and the giving of medical advice with respect to their use. Although it is commonly supposed that the Catholic Church is responsible for this legislation, a study of its history indicates that its original enactment reflected Protestant morality of the Anthony Comstock era. The validity of this legislation was argued before the Supreme Court wholly in terms of whether this was a valid exercise of the police power. Unfortunately, the outcome of the case was not decisive. A majority held that it was unnecessary to reach a decision since the statute was not being enforced, hence the constitutional issue was avoided.[22] Two judges believing that there was a case for the exercise of the judicial power found the statute invalid as an arbitrary restriction on individual liberty.[23] The avoidance by the majority of the constitutional issue suggests that they did recognize a substantial constitutional question presented by this kind of legislation. Two dissenters made clear that in their opinion there were no adequate considerations of public interest or policy to warrant this restriction on personal liberty. The notable dissent written by Justice Harlan stressed the argument that the statute in prohibiting use of contraceptives sanctioned a drastic invasion of the privacy of the home and of the marital relationship. Here, then, is the key to the general problem under consideration. Legislation identifiable with religious views and practices is constitutional if it can be supported by adequate considerations of a secular or civil nature relevant to the exercise of governmental power. Otherwise, it fails either as an attempt to establish religion or simply as an arbitrary exercise of power unrelated to appropriate public objectives.

In the situation just discussed, the problem is whether government through the exercise of its police power is attempting to establish a religion, that is, whether by means of regulation of behavior compelling people to abstain from certain conduct it is sanctioning the views of a particular religion. The impact on personal liberty is evident in this case, and the standing of a person affected by this to raise the question whether this is an attempt to establish religion is clear also. The more frequently arising question in respect to the establishment of religion concerns the spending by a state of money or the use of public property for purposes which are said to aid religion or to favor a religion and thereby to violate the establishment idea. These are probably the most pressing questions we face at the present time. Thus, the question arises with respect to use of government funds for the purpose of aiding parochial schools in one way or another.

It should be noted that as soon as we get into questions with respect to the use of public funds, property, or facilities in aid of religion, we also get into an important remedial and standing question. The remedial and standing question is, in turn, related to the meritorious question of underlying constitutional right, particularly when we are talking about the application of the Fourteenth Amendment. No person can claim that he is being deprived of life, liberty, or property without due process of law by reference to allegedly unconstitutional use of state funds in support of or by way of establishment of religion unless he can demonstrate some substantial injury to life, liberty, or property. If a special tax is levied in order to support a church establishment, this clearly gives the taxpayer standing by virtue of the financial imposition made upon him. Or if in connection with the use of funds to support religious education, where it is not clear that there is a substantial use of these funds or any out-of-pocket charges against the government, the attempt is made to force this program on some unwilling person, it is clear here, too, that because of this invasion of his own freedom of conscience, he has standing to raise the question. But unless a person can demonstrate that alleged governmental participation or involvement in or support of some program alleged to aid religion is a substantial diversion of tax funds and thereby burdens him as a taxpayer or otherwise infringes upon his own freedom, it is not clear that he has standing to raise these questions.[24]

This point is particularly worth noting in respect to attempts to question the validity of spending by the federal government. In the well-known case of *Frothingham* v. *Mellon*[25] the Supreme Court held that a federal taxpayer as such does not have standing to raise questions in respect to the validity of federal spending. This case was decided on the theory that a taxpayer has such a small and remote interest in funds in the federal treasury that he cannot claim any personal damage because funds derived from tax sources are being used in an unconstitutional way. We need not emphasize the importance of this idea in respect to questions that may be raised with respect to the validity of federal spending for parochial schools, for instance. Even if we had a clear case of appropriation of funds by the federal government to aid religion or to aid religious education as religious education, it is not clear at this point just who could raise the question. If *Frothingham* v. *Mellon* were followed in this situation, taxpayers would not have standing. It may be that because of the importance of the First Amendment restriction the Court will permit tax-payers to question any spending of money which is alleged to result in an establishment of religion. This remains to be seen. At this point it is enough to note that the standing problem presents substantial difficulties.

In taking a closer look at the questions raised in regard to use of public funds, facilities, or property as a means of aiding religion and thereby constituting an unlawful establishment, several general considerations may be noted at the outset.

In the first place, notwithstanding what has been said by the Supreme Court, particularly in its dictum in the *Everson* case, the truth and the historical fact are that government funds have been spent distinctively in support of religious purposes. Although Justice Frankfurter said in his concurring opinion in the Sunday closing law cases that government can never do anything that will support or endorse any religious view or views, history does not support so sweeping an assertion. The clearest case in refutation of this is the use of federal funds to pay salaries to officers in the armed forces who are military chaplains and whose whole function is to perform a religious ministry to men in the armed services. Now we know that some special reasons are given for this situation, namely, that men in the armed forces are away from their usual homes and environment where they have the opportunity to attend the church of their choice and so the government is meeting this need by supplying a chaplain service and this, in turn, is related to the government's interest in maintaining the morale and well-being of its soldiers. In other words, the government does have a proper and valid interest here that warrants the expen-diture of funds for this kind of religious ministry. Whatever the special reasons given, at least this demonstrates an important consideration, namely, that any absolutes in respect to nonuse of public funds to aid religion simply do not fit the case. The problems in this area cannot be solved by condemning all recognition of religious purposes or assistance for religious purposes as being unconstitutional. At present there is a movement in force in many of the states to supply chaplains at state institutions such as penitentiaries, hospitals, and the like. Again, no one seems seriously to question the validity of spending for this purpose even though it is distinctively in aid of a religious purpose. In this connection we may mention also the granting of tax exemptions for property used for religious purposes or for purposes of religious education. No one can doubt that this amounts to substantial financial assistance by the state to religious institutions. Again, a rationalization is offered to justify this situation, namely, that since exemption for church property is usually part of a statutory pattern whereby exemption is allowed for various types of properties used for nonprofit purposes, therefore, it is appropriate to permit this exemption for property used for religious purposes, otherwise there would be a discrimination against one class of property owned and operated by nonprofit institutions. This seems to be a tenable theory, but acquiescence in this theory should not obscure the fact that tax exemptions are generally recognized to be valid because the underlying institutions serve a proper public purpose and in many instances they perform functions which otherwise the state would have to perform. I am not suggesting that the justification for tax exemptions for churches is that they are performing a function which the state otherwise would perform, but I am suggesting that an exemption here is a recognition of the fact that religious institutions do serve a sufficiently public purpose to warrant this kind of treatment.

A second consideration that deserves emphasis is that under some circumstances a state may have to make a choice between the principle that it cannot aid religion on the one hand and the competing principle that it cannot discriminate against religion. Perhaps this is already illustrated in the tax exemption case previously cited, where it may be said that if tax exemptions are granted to all nonprofit institutions, it would be an unwarranted discrimination to deny the exemption to one particular class of nonprofit institutions, namely, churches and church-operated schools. Perhaps an even better illustration is found in the cases involving the use of public properties for purposes of religious meetings. The numerous cases involving Jehovah's Witnesses furnish an excellent illustration of this period. According to the Supreme Court's decisions there is a right to use public ways, including streets and sidewalks and public parks, for purposes of religious meetings and demonstrations as well as for other public meeting purposes. This is based on the theory in these cases of the free exercise of religion.[26] It cannot be doubted that in these cases the state by making its facilities available—and it is told that it is under a constitutional duty to do so—is aiding religion and is aiding the free exercise of religion. Yet not only is this permissible as a form of aid to religion, but it is even constitutionally required.

Finally, I revert to the idea that a concurrence of function may be found in some cases, so far as the separate functions of both church and state are concerned. In the Sunday closing law cases the Court recognized that although it can be said the Christian church has a special interest in observance of Sunday, the state has a concurrent interest in having all people observe a day of rest and it may appropriately choose Sunday as the designated day for this purpose. Here we have a concurrence of religious and secular interest converging upon the same result. There may also be a concurrence of interest with respect to the performance of certain functions, where the question is properly raised whether because of such concurrence of interest a state may appropriately recognize and support certain undertakings carried on by the churches. It is useful to note in this connection that a notable aspect of the secularization of American life is the gradual taking over by the state of many functions at one time performed by the churches. We do recognize that it is appropriately a religious function to engage in activities other than having church services on Sunday. It is appropriately a church function to operate hospitals, to operate schools and colleges, and to take care of the needs of orphans and old people and of the needy and helpless. Yet we know also that in these areas the state has been moving in more and more, and that with the progressive acceptance of the conception of the welfare state or the social service state we are looking to government to perform functions which at one time were performed wholly or primarily by the churches. The fact that the state is now performing these functions in no way impairs the validity of the churches' performance of these same functions.

The question then arises, however, whether because of concurrence of interests and objectives the state may to some extent support these functions when carried on by the church. At this point we may choose simply for illustrative purposes the operation of hospitals. Clearly, the operation of hospitals is a public function warranting the use of public funds. On the other hand, churches have traditionally operated hospitals as means of ministering to the sick and of expressing the concern and compassion of the church. Is it appropriate for government in any way to subsidize the operations of privately owned and operated hospitals including hospitals owned and operated by the churches? The question is probably academic because we know this has been done under the federal Hill-Burton Act[27] whereby benefit of these funds to assist in the construction of new and additional hospital facilities has been extended to hospitals owned and operated by church groups. The theory here is that the government is supporting these hospitals obviously not because they are religious institutions but because they are performing a function which the state itself can perform.[28]

Government and Religious Education

We turn our attention now to the questions raised in respect to the relationship between the government and education and, more particularly, questions raised in respect to government and religious education. In general, it can be said that two underlying questions are presented by current developments and both of them have to do with the problem of establishment of religion by the state. The first is the question whether or not the state may in any way support any kind of program of religion in the public schools. The second is the question whether the state may give any form of assistance to the operation of parochial schools.

The problem in respect to religious education or religious exercise in state-supported educational institutions presents distinctive aspects, depending on the level of education involved. In dealing with this problem first of all at the public school level, is it appropriate to include as part of a public school program the reading of the Bible and even the recitation in unison of the Lord's Prayer? I think it can hardly be doubted that the introduction of Bible reading and prayer exercise at the beginning of the school day is intended to have a religious significance, and it is difficult to avoid the conclusion that this does favor a particular religion, notably the Christian religion, and more particularly the Protestant religion, depending on the version of the Bible that is used. As mentioned at the beginning of this chapter, the public schools for many years reflected a primary Protestant orientation, and the practice of opening sessions with Bible readings and even recitation of the Lord's Prayer reflects this Protestant influence.

It is perhaps noteworthy that these practices frequently come under attack not from antireligionists but from religionists such as Catholics and Jews, who contend that this is an attempt to use the public schools for purposes of inculcating Protestantism in the students. Historically, the Bible-reading practice has been widespread, and if history is any index to the meaning of the Fourteenth Amendment, it would be difficult to deny the validity of this practice. However, in view of the pronouncements by the Supreme Court in recent years on the meaning of the First Amendment which is also read into the Fourteenth Amendment, it would be very difficult to support the validity of such practices at present. The circumstances under which these exercises are conducted by a public school teacher—on school premises and as part of the regular school day—all point to the conclusion that the state through the use of its facilities, personnel, and regular program is engaging directly in instruction and exercises that have a primary religious motivation and significance and which tend to favor one religious group.[29] It must be kept in mind that a person who objects must have a substantial basis of standing to do so either by showing that he is a taxpayer and that tax funds are being used in an unlawful way—a very difficult thing to maintain here because of difficulty of showing out-of-pocket expenditure funds—or that his own liberty or that of his children is being infringed upon and in that case some actual coercive effect must be demonstrated.[30] The point should be observed also that the reading and study of the Bible as litera- ture, or the study of religion, or instruction in moral values and ethics are not objectionable so long as they are not identified with exercises and activities aimed at the cultivation of religious faith or motivation. Moreover, the Supreme Court has held that school boards may permit released time for religious in- struction by teachers supplied by religious groups, provided this does not take place on the school premises.[31]

By contrast we may point to the situation existing in many state universities, where in various ways courses in religion are included as a part of the curriculum, either as courses included in particular departments or in a separate school of religion as at the State University of Iowa.[32] Here very clearly is the use of public funds to support an interest in religion and to support teaching in the field of religion. No one seems seriously to ques- tion the validity of this practice even though it does show that any sweeping assertions about the invalidity and use of money to support religious education must be examined with a good deal of care and skepticism. The real reasons for distin- guishing this situation from that of the public schools are that attendance at state universities is voluntary, participation in these particular courses dealing with religion is voluntary, and the greater maturity of the student precludes any notion that this is an attempt to indoctrinate or to compel students to accept a particular religious belief.[33] This distinction between the two situations again points up a very important conclusion, namely, that the broad assertion made in the interpretation of the First Amendment that no public funds can be used to aid religion in any way, or that it is even inappropriate for the state to show any kind of affirmative interest in the matter of religion or religious instruction, is not supported by history or by present practice.

The problems get more difficult when we get into questions relating to the use of public funds in support of educational institutions owned and operated by churches, whether it be parochial schools operated at the primary and secondary level or colleges owned and operated by churches. In those cases the religious environment and religious objectives assume an integral significance in the total educational process.

In respect to the problem generating the greatest amount of current controversy, the question is raised whether in the event of federal aid to education it would be appropriate to assist private as well as public schools, including in the private category schools operated by churches and commonly known as parochial schools. It should be emphasized that we are concerned here wholly with limitations derived from the First Amendment. Specific provisions of some state constitutions limiting the use of public funds have a more restrictive effect on the power of state legislatures in spending money in aid of parochial schools than general limitations derived from the First Amendment.

The problem grows immediately out of the proposal that the federal government assist the states in the operation of the public school system by making grants to be administered through the states for the purpose of aiding the schools either in construction of new facilities or in meeting annual operating expenses.[34] Essentially, the idea is that the federal government will tap its own financial resources in order to return to the states some of the money collected from federal taxpayers in order to help the states in operating their schools. The question that arises is whether or not the federal government should, as part of this program, give some financial assistance also to parochial schools. This is the immediate question. Interesting questions are raised also by the part of the President's program relating to colleges, including church-related colleges.

The position of the administration as stated by President Kennedy has been that constitutionally the federal government can give assistance only to public schools operated by the states and that to aid parochial schools by any kind of federal financial assistance would violate the First Amendment as interpreted in the *Everson* case.[35] In opposition to this view has been the position—asserted chiefly by the Catholic hierarchy—that while it may be constitutionally objectionable to use federal funds to support parochial schools in the same measure as public schools, it would not be unconstitutional for the federal government to make loans at relatively low interest rates in order to assist parochial schools to meet their capital needs either by way of building new schools or extending or improving present facilities.[36]

It should be evident from what has already been said that the constitutional question respecting federal aid for parochial schools does not admit of the easy or ready answer given by some who are opposed to such aid.

Education is not a matter falling within the primary and direct jurisdiction of the federal government. At most, general education, as distinguished from education for certain specific purposes,[37] comes within the reach of the federal government's authority by virtue of its power to spend for the general welfare.[38] The theory in support of Congressional spending for general education is that Congress may determine that this contribution to the more effective functioning of the nation's educational system—by aiding the construction of more and better physical facilities and the payment of higher teachers' salaries—will promote the nation's general welfare.

If "general welfare" is the only consideration, no substantial difficulty is raised about the use of federal funds to aid parochial as well as public education, since attendance at these schools satisfies the compulsory school attendance laws of the several states and thereby serves the public purpose and objectives underlying these laws.[39] The constitutional issue that is raised is not whether this is spending for the general welfare but rather whether it is prohibited by the First Amendment's nonestablishment clause. Quite clearly, if either the federal government or the states were to provide money to aid Sunday school education or to provide transportation for children attending Sunday school, this would be the kind of support of religion prohibited by the nonestablishment clause. The problem is quite different, however, when we talk about schools which are operated by churches but which parallel the public school system. Two important considerations must be emphasized. First, compulsory school laws place a duty on parents to send their children to a school that meets the state's educational standards and requirements. The public interest in having all children receive a minimum education—an objective that is vital and indispensable to a democratic society —furnishes the justification for these compulsory education laws. Any schools, including parochial schools, that satisfy the state's requirements thereby serve the public purpose underlying the compulsory education laws. Since a parent cannot receive credit for discharging his statutory obligation unless the school to which he sends his child meets the state's requirements by reference to secular courses that are taught, minimum number of school days, health and safety standards, and qualification of teachers, it is evident that private schools by meeting these requirements are already integrated in a substantial way into the total educational system within a state.

Secondly, these schools outside the public school system, but serving the same purpose under the compulsory school laws as the state-owned and operated schools, do not exist by sufferance or tolerance of the state. This is an important consideration. In the famous *Pierce* case[40] the Supreme Court held that it is a constitutional right of parents to send children to the school of their choice, so long as the school meets requirements and standards that the state may properly impose, and that a state statute compelling parents to send their children to public schools is unconstitutional. By virtue of this decision churches have a right to operate schools and parents have a right to send their children to parochial schools. The Court in sustaining these fundamental rights placed a constitutional barrier in the path of state monopoly of the educational process and of a state-directed program of forcing all students into the mold of a uniform secular educational process. If parents wish to send their children to a school where religion assumes significance as a unifying element in the total educational program, this is their right. The public school is a cherished symbol of our democracy, but it may also be suggested that parochial and nonparochial private schools, having their own important constitutional status and representing a basic freedom of choice on the part of parents, are an equally important and impressive symbol of our democratic and pluralistic culture. This is worth noting since it seems to me that so much of the opposition to aid for parochial schools stems from a feeling against these schools as though there were something almost un-American about them.

The discussion here is not focused on the merits of the public schools versus parochial schools or on the policy considerations, pro and con, respecting use of public funds to aid parochial schools. We are concerned here with the constitutional aspects of any program of federal aid to education that includes assistance for parochial as well as public and nonparochial private schools. If the federal government were to make loans to churches to assist in the construction of new or additional school facilities, would this be the kind of "aid to religion" or support of religious education which according to the dictum of the *Everson* case is unconstitutional as an attempt to establish religion?

The Supreme Court has already sustained the use of public tax funds to transport children to parochial as well as public schools on the theory that this is not really aid to religious education but social welfare legislation.[41] It is apparent that the solution to some of these problems depends on placing the right label on the legislative program, and that if we can label a particular program as social or child welfare rather than aid to religious education, we thereby determine the constitutional result. And even before the *Everson* case, the Court had held that the distribution of secular textbooks to children in parochial schools did not violate any constitutional limitations.[42] This was even more direct aid to education conducted under the auspices of a church. But the distribution of these books served a valid secular purpose.

Other instances of assistance that have not reached the courts may be cited: perhaps the most notable is the free lunch program under the sponsorship of the federal government.[43] Children are not denied the benefits of this because they are attending a parochial as distinguished from a public school. Here the theory is that this is a child benefit program and that this is not direct assistance to religious education. The test propounded by some is whether the assistance is a direct subsidy to church bodies to aid them in the operation of their schools or whether it is a so-called fringe benefit that does not reach the heart of the educational process. The National Defense Education Act of 1958[44] made funds available to colleges and high schools to assist in the acquisition of new equipment needed for the study of science, mathematics, and foreign languages. Under the authority of this statute, federal funds have been loaned to parochial high schools.[45]

It is said, however, that neither bus transportation, distribution of secular textbooks, the free lunch program, or use of funds for laboratory equipment involves the state in support of a program of coerced religious instruction—a matter beyond the competence of the state to direct or support. The difficulty with this interpretation is that it leaves the critical question unanswered. At what point can it be said that financial assistance to parochial schools can be so identified with religious instruction as to make it an unconstitutional establishment? There can be no precise answer to this. If the relevant cases—those dealing with bus transportation and textbooks—furnish any answer at all, it is that the state can afford some support for parochial schools insofar as they discharge the same secular functions as the public schools even though they have the plus element of religion. In other words, the concurrence of function principle is applicable here. The parochial schools do serve a recognized public purpose so far as the state's total interest in the educational process is concerned.

By emphasis on the secular aspects of parochial school education, substantial financial assistance can be given without running into the obstacle that it amounts to an establishment of religion. If any distinguishing limitation is to be observed, it is that over-all subsidies to parochial schools, which include support for operating expenses, are invalid because they further the teaching of religion, whereas assistance for specific purposes not directly and immediately identified with religious

instruction is valid and proper.[46] In line with this theory a
case may be made to support the validity of a program of federal
loans to assist in the construction of new parochial school facilities. Buildings, like buses and laboratory equipment, are
neutral or can even be labeled secular.[47] At least there is no
controlling precedent that would require a conclusion that
such use of federal funds would be unconstitutional.

The opposition in some quarters to any assistance from
federal funds for parochial school education is all the more
striking in view of the apparent acquiescence in proposals for
assistance to higher education that raise parallel questions.
Thus, President Kennedy's proposed aid-to-education program
calls not only for a continuation of loans to colleges, including
church colleges, for self-liquidating projects such as dormitories, but also for a new program of grants to colleges, including church colleges, for academic buildings. It likewise
calls for tuition scholarships for students going to private
colleges and an additional grant of $300 to the institution
itself on the theory that the cost of tuition is not commensurate
with the total cost of educating the student. A program of loans
to colleges on a long-term basis at cheap interest rates to help
build dormitories, cafeterias, and other buildings has been in
effect now for several years,[48] but it has not excited any major
constitutional arguments. Yet can it be questioned that the use
of this government money at low interest rates is a financial
aid to these colleges, many of which are under the control of
church bodies? The low interest rate in effect frees operating
expenses that may go into other phases of the college program.
The President's further proposal of grants to colleges by the
federal government for the construction of educational buildings would have the same effect. A similar problem is raised
with respect to grants to church-related colleges to supplement

tuition scholarships given to students who attend those colleges. Here are grants to be made directly to institutions to aid in their educational programs. Yet in many church-related colleges, religion is just as central a part of the educational program and objectives as it is in parochial schools.

As previously noted, a distinction is observed in practice between religion in the public schools and in state universities, and the position is taken that a parallel distinction can and should be made on the issue of spending federal funds to support church-related colleges as opposed to public schools, and that consistent with the nonestablishment restriction the federal government may aid private colleges, including church-related colleges, either by direct grants or loans or by benefit grants to students in a way not permitted with respect to parochial schools. In support of this position it is argued that private institutions play a much larger role in the total scheme of higher education as contrasted to the place of parochial schools in the over-all system of primary and secondary education, that the state colleges and universities cannot take care of all the students who want a college education, that there is no compulsion to attend college, that the states do not provide tuition-free education at the higher level, that religion is a less conspicuous feature of church-related colleges as contrasted to parochial schools, and that the college student's greater maturity limits the opportunity for sectarian indoctrination.[49] Whether or not these arguments are adequately supported, and whether or not they furnish a satisfactory and persuasive basis for distinction in respect to the constitutional issues raised respecting federal aid to parochial schools and church-related colleges, respectively, at least it is clear that these distinctions rest wholly on practical, pragmatic, and functional considerations as a guide to interpretation of the First Amendment limitation.

In any event, it is clear that the government may give some support to parochial school education, either by way of so-called fringe benefits or by subsidizing particular phases of this education identifiable as secular in character. A principal reason justifying these expenditures is that parochial schools do serve a secular as well as religious purpose. But we may also stress another reason, and this is that the state in giving some assistance to parochial schools is thereby making a meaningful contribution in support of the right of parents to send children to the school of their choice. It may at a point become an empty gesture to talk about this right or about the correlative privilege of churches and other bodies or groups to operate schools, along with the public school system, if the cost to parents of maintaining these private schools, in addition to the burden of supporting the public schools, is so great that as a practical matter it can no longer be borne. This is not to suggest that the government is under a constitutional duty to support private schools in whole or in part. I do not believe there is any such duty. But the constitutional right of parents to send children to a school of their own choice, particularly when this choice is dictated by religious considerations, is a substantial factor to be considered in any discussion of the problem. There are situations where choices must be made between the policy underlying the free exercise of religion and the policy of nonestablishment of religion. For Congress to decide that it will encourage the free exercise of religion by limited capital grants or loans to parochial schools at the expense of some aid to religion would not be an arbitrary choice, where in making this choice Congress also advances the general welfare served by the nation's total educational program and the secular objectives of the state's compulsory education laws.

I am not advocating federal aid for parochial schools. But

it is my opinion that consistent with the nonestablishment principle of the First Amendment and the separation limitation derived from it, and in view of the interpretations given to this language and the practices that have been sanctioned, Congress may grant some assistance to these schools as part of a program of spending for the general welfare, so long as the funds are so limited and their expenditure so directed as not to be a direct subsidy for religious teaching.

I am satisfied that we cannot find answers to any of the questions in the field of church-state relations by employing broad and sweeping postulates based on a theory of complete separation or on a theory that the state can do nothing which in fact aids religion. These problems will have to be answered on a pragmatic basis that takes account of competing and conflicting interests and of the underlying purposes served by the separation principle. But it should also be stressed that the issue of constitutional power should not be confused with the question whether it is desirable or wise as a matter of policy for the government to give support to parochial schools. Certainly, any proposal for such support does involve very important policy considerations. On the one hand, the effect of such assistance in promoting parochial schools and the resulting impact and effect on the public school system must be considered and weighed. And, in turn, those interested in the parochial schools must seriously and carefully weigh the question whether and to what extent they should receive and accept assistance from the government at the expense of submission to controls that properly accompany grants of public funds. But these are questions of policy to be debated and argued in the public forum and in the legislative halls. Debate on these issues should not be foreclosed or obscured by indiscriminate invocation of the separation principle derived from the First Amendment.

II. OBSCENITY AND CENSORSHIP: PROTECTING THE PUBLIC MORALS

Legislative concern for the protection of public morals is no new phenomenon in American life. It is classic black letter learning that the police power may appropriately be exercised to protect the public morals as well as public health and safety and the general welfare. New attention has been focused on the subject, however, as the result of developments of recent years. Because of the large-scale production and circulation of cheap and trashy paperbacks and comics featuring crime, violence, and sex, of a steady stream of pornographic pictures through the mails, and of the exhibition of films exploiting sex in a cheap way and with suggestive effects, legislators and law enforcement officers, reflecting a heightened sense of public concern over what is feared to be a corrupting influence on the moral thinking and conduct of the community and particularly of young people, have moved in the direction of a more vigorous program for dealing with publications of this kind. On the other hand, the Supreme Court, in response to these efforts to protect the public morals, has taken a new look at the constitutional guarantee of freedom of the press as it is affected by enforcement of obscenity legislation and the administration of movie censorship laws.

The campaign against literature deemed to be obscene or otherwise objectionable because of its depiction of scenes of crime and violence has taken several forms. Criminal prosecutions have been brought against book dealers for selling obscene books. In some cases a special statutory procedure permits an injunction against the further circulation of books found in a judicial proceeding to be obscene. The post office department has been waging a vigorous campaign through the powers given to it to halt the circulation of what the post office considers to be pornographic material. In a number of states and communities pursuant to local ordinance and statutory authorization, no movie may be exhibited unless it is first submitted for examination by a censorship board which has authority to deny permission for its exhibition if it is found to violate certain statutory standards.

The new emphasis in constitutional litigation is reflected in the important decisions of the Supreme Court on the question whether the federal government and the states may enforce legislation prescribing punishment for the distribution and sale of obscene literature and the related cases dealing with the problem of remedial measures, including sanctions directed against book dealers. Also important is the decision by the Court during the past term when for the first time it came to grips with the question whether movie censorship by a state or a political subdivision of the state is in itself unconstitutional as an abridgment of freedom of the press. The currency of these questions makes it desirable to review this general area and more particularly to discuss the significance of the recent decisions and their implications.

Free Press and Constitutional Limitations

The First Amendment prohibits Congress from making any law abridging the freedom of the press. This language is categorical and appears on the surface to state a solid prohibition on the power of Congress to use its delegated powers in a way which results in any abridgment of the liberty encompassed within the freedom of the press. Any limitation on the state with respect to freedom of the press must be derived from the Fourteenth Amendment and more particularly from the clause of the Fourteenth Amendment which provides that no state shall deprive any person of liberty without due process of law. Inasmuch as the questions in respect to a state's restrictions on freedom of the press are usually raised by persons such as movie exhibitors, newspaper corporations, and book publishers and dealers, it may be argued with some persuasiveness that what is involved is equally a question of deprivation of economic liberty and of property without due process of law, since restrictions on the publication, sale, and circulation of books and movies operate as a limitation on their freedom to do business.

Consistent with the classical interpretation of the Fourteenth Amendment whereby the Due Process Clause has emerged as a vehicle for the judicial protection of so-called fundamental liberties against arbitrary state impairment, the Court beginning with the famous case of *Near* v. *Minnesota*[1] found that freedom of the press was such a fundamental liberty subject to protection under the Fourteenth Amendment. In a host of later decisions the Court has built upon this idea in protecting freedom of the press against state and local action. It should also be noted at this point that the Supreme Court has also said at various times that the Fourteenth Amendment incorporates the First Amendment freedoms.[2] Indeed, some members of the Court have said from time to time that the effect of the Fourteenth Amendment is to make the Bill of Rights applicable to the states.[3] The question whether the First Amendment does apply directly to the states through the Fourteenth, in the sense that states are limited in dealing with the press in the same way that Congress is, assumes critical importance in discussion of these questions.[4] If we are dealing with the question only of whether a person has been deprived of liberty or property without due process of law, then the familiar due process considerations apply, namely, that liberty and property are subject to limitations in the general exercise of the states' police powers so long as the legislation is directed toward reasonable ends and employs reasonable means, as determined within the discretion of the legislature, for achieving these ends. On the other hand, in view of the categorical language of the First Amendment and the ideas expressed at various times that the First Amendment freedoms are preferred freedoms, that the validity of legislation impinging upon these freedoms will not be presumed, that the Court will more closely scrutinize any restrictions on these freedoms, and that the Court will not indulge in the usual deference to legislative judgment, a substantially different approach is indicated if the states are limited by the First Amendment and not by the Due Process Clause. Indeed, according to some justices of the Supreme Court the freedoms of the First Amendment are absolute within the sphere of their application.[5] In any event the limitations imposed on the power of the states to restrict freedom of the press will depend then on the validity of the incorporation theory and the extent to which First Amendment freedoms are more effectively protected by the Court than the freedoms resting solely on the Due Process Clause.

Since its key decision in *Near* v. *Minnesota,* which, it may be noted, rested on the Due Process Clause and not on the First Amendment, the Court has in a variety of situations upheld freedom of the press either as a fundamental liberty under the Fourteenth Amendment or as a freedom protected

by the First Amendment as against restriction imposed by the
states. Thus, a state tax levied on a newspaper's advertising
receipts was deemed to be repressive and invalid as a tax on
the press.[6] In a series of cases the Court has found that contempt decrees issued by state courts against newspapers for
allegedly contemptuous publications violated freedom of the
press.[7] Indeed, in these cases the Court relied on the use of
the clear-and-present-danger formula as a means of checking
and testing the validity of judicial contempt orders. Freedom
of the press emerged as the central issue in a whole series of
cases dealing with the validity of municipal ordinances that
place restrictions on the freedom to distribute and circulate
literature of various kinds. In the key case, *Lovell* v. *City of
Griffin*,[8] the Court found that an ordinance which required
that a person secure the permission of the chief of police in
order to distribute literature in a public place was invalid
because it operated as a prior restraint on freedom to circulate
literature. But the prior restraint idea has not been the sole
factor here. Ordinances making it punishable to distribute
literature have been held invalid on the same ground.[9] In
some of these cases, perhaps the majority of them, the Court
has been dealing with Jehovah's Witnesses, and the decision
has been based on religious freedom rather than freedom of
the press. In this connection it is interesting to note that the
Court has observed a distinction between solicitation of sales
of religious literature, as part of a program of religious propaganda activities, and solicitation of sales of other types of
literature. Thus, a municipal ordinance of the Green River
type prohibiting the ringing of doorbells for the purpose of
soliciting sales is valid when enforced against agents for
such magazines as the *Saturday Evening Post*,[10] although the

Court has invalidated a similar restraint with respect to Jehovah's Witnesses soliciting sales of their literature.[11]

In still another series of cases the Court found freedom of expression involved in attempts by state courts to interfere with the freedom of picketing. Picketing has been viewed as a form of expression designed to convey certain ideas to the public and thus has come within the protection of the free press guarantee.[12] Most of these cases arising in the past dealt with labor problems, and despite the Court's early position in which it invalidated a number of judicial decrees interfering with picketing in labor cases, the later decisions have taken a much more moderate position and have recognized that picketing may be restrained in order to serve appropriate public interests.[13] Indeed, in these cases we have seen the rise and decline of one particular phase of what may be described as the free press idea.

Basic Principles Established by Judicial Interpretation

It is against the background of this general judicial development in the exposition of the free press idea that we take a closer look at the particular problems with which we are concerned, namely, problems generated by obscenity and censorship legislation. But before doing this it may be helpful to summarize briefly some basic ideas developed by the judicial decisions surveyed in the preceding discussion.

1. Freedom of the press is recognized as a liberty protected against state impairment under the Fourteenth Amendment whether on the theory that it is a right which is fundamental to the concept of ordered justice and liberty or on the theory that the liberty phrasing of the Due Process Clause incorporates the freedoms of the First Amendment.

2. Freedom of the press is not an absolute right and may be subjected to restraints and limitations designed to protect appropriate private or public interests. It is elementary doctrine, of course, that a person who publishes a libelous statement may properly be subjected to a civil suit for damages or to a criminal libel prosecution and that in these proceedings he cannot stand upon freedom of the press as a basis of immunity for his action that has resulted in harm to others. Moreover, the Court in *Beauharnais v. Illinois*[14] sanctioned state antihate legislation which imposed criminal sanctions on persons guilty of publishing statements which exposed the citizens of any race, color, creed, or religion to contempt, derision, or obloquy. The Court viewed this as a reasonable extension of the basic principle underlying the law of libel and justified by familiar police power considerations. Any attempt at rationalization of the legislation directed against libelous publications reveals either of two general processes employed by the Court, and the choice of either process depends again on whether, so far as the states are concerned, the question is entirely one of due process of law or whether the question is governed by the First Amendment as incorporated in the Fourteenth.

Viewed as a due process problem, so that any right claimed is subject to a reasonable exercise of the police power, there is, of course, no difficulty in sustaining the restraints on freedom of the press that result from the law of libel. Both the history of these matters and the nature of the interests sought to be protected warrant the exercise of the police power to impose sanctions against those who injure others by exercising their freedom. This was the approach of the majority in the *Beauharnais* case. On the other hand, if the approach is made in terms of the First Amendment and if the interpretation of

the First Amendment is that within the sphere of its operation it imposes a complete limitation on the legislative power
to abridge freedom of the press, justification for criminal libel
legislation must depend on the Court's interpretation of
freedom of the press. Here a definitional or conceptual approach determines the answer. If we say that historically libel
is not included in the freedom of the press idea, then antilibel
legislation has no protection under the First Amendment.
Similarly, if it can be said that the use of so-called "fighting
words" by way of epithets does not come within the free press
guarantee, legislation directed against the use of such words
raises no problem under the First Amendment.[15] It seems
clear that the Court must engage in many of the same
processes that characterize the due process technique in determining the basic definitional issue of whether a given type
of speech falls within the language protected under the First
Amendment. In short, the due process approach under the
Fourteenth Amendment in terms of the reasonable exercise
of the police power and the definitional approach under the
First Amendment may converge in some cases to reach the
same result.

Even if a particular type of publication is deemed to come
within the free press guarantee of the First Amendment, it does
not follow that some restriction on this freedom is prohibited
to Congress. It is true that the absolutists on the Court would
invalidate any abridgment of free press. But a present majority of the Court hold that First Amendment freedoms are not
absolute and that Congressional restriction on these freedoms
is constitutional if on balance it appears that the public interest
advanced or secured by the legislation outweighs in importance
the resulting restriction on individual freedom.[16] What was
said earlier about the substantial differences between applying

a Fourteenth Amendment due process theory and a First Amendment freedom theory in passing on the validity of restrictive state legislation loses much of its significance once it is conceded that the First Amendment freedoms are not absolute and that they must be weighed in the balance against competing public interests. In terms of judicial technique and judicial self-restraint, the application of the standard of reasonableness as an index to due process of law involves basically a consideration of the same underlying factors employed in the balance-of-interest approach, although in theory the bare rationality test under the Due Process Clause involves less judicial scrutinizing and weighing of competing interests than the balance-of-interest technique. In any event, whether we talk about an absolute freedom under the First Amendment within the scope of the guarantee, whether we talk about a balancing of First Amendment freedoms against appropriate public interests served by restrictive legislation, or whether we are talking about the reasonable exercise of the police power consistent with due process of law under the Fourteenth Amendment, the same results are reached in some of these cases, and the practical effect and conclusion to be drawn are that freedom of the press as used in the general sense is not an absolute or unconditional freedom.

3. It is clear from the cases that the validity of a legislative limitation on freedom of press may depend upon the type of restraint imposed. This brings us to the well-recognized distinction between prior and post restraints. Admittedly, there is some fuzziness in the application of these distinctions, and the term prior restraint may often be used in such a way as to destroy its essential and historic meaning. Historically, it would appear that prior restraint on publication means that some prior approval must be obtained from a governmental

agency before a person can publish or circulate a book, periodical, or pamphlet. In other words, prior restraint in its classical sense has reference to a system of censorship, and this term is usually understood to refer to a system of governmental regulation whereby official approval must be secured in advance of publication. On the other hand, post restraint has reference to the imposition of sanctions and remedies that arise after an initial publication. Thus, a criminal libel law is a post restraint, and a civil action at law for damages for publication of libelous material is a post restraint. The important distinction between the two lies, of course, in the consideration that a system of post restraint at least does permit an expression of ideas for what they may be worth so that the public can read and judge, but with the imposition of responsibility on the publisher for damage he has caused to public or private interest. The deterrent effect of a post restraint, however, may be such that it operates with the same effect as a prior restraint. If the sanctions imposed for a criminal libel or any civil proceeding become so heavy that they operate to harass and discourage the free expression of ideas, the practical effect may be that of prior restraint. We mention this only to suggest that the difference between post and prior restraint is perhaps in terms of consequence and result and the corresponding limitation on freedom of the press more a matter of degree rather than a real difference in kind. Moreover, the distinction may be observed between prior restraint on initial publication and prior restraint on distribution and circulation after initial publication. Thus, if a book that has been published is found to be libelous or to be obscene following a notice of hearing and a judicial determination to this effect, an injunction directed against further circulation requiring destruction of these books does impose a prior restraint in the sense that no further distribution is permitted. It is a prior restraint but it originates at a point in time later than the kind of prior restraint that lays a hand on publication in the first instance. This is a case where, to borrow a homely analogy, we may say, assuming we make a distinction here for constitutional purposes, that every dog is entitled to one bite. According to this theory, every book is entitled to see the light of day and to have at least one purchaser, and every film is entitled to see the light of day and to have at least one showing. After that, pursuant to notice and hearing, further circulation may be barred.

Whatever may be the definitional difficulties involved in distinguishing between prior and post restraints, at least it is clear that the Supreme Court has over the years beginning with the *Near* case[17] attached the greatest importance to freedom from prior restraint. The state statute involved in the *Near* case declared a "malicious, scandalous and defamatory" newspaper to be a public nuisance and authorized a court to issue an appropriate order, after a hearing, requiring abatement of the offending newspaper. In this case the court enjoined the defendants from publishing any malicious, scandalous, or defamatory newspaper and from further conducting the nuisance as established by prior publications of their newspaper. Actually, there was no prior restraint in the usual sense, since the newspaper was subject to restraint only after repeated publication supported the finding that it was a nuisance. Moreover, even after a newspaper was declared to be a nuisance, general publication was not enjoined. But the further publication of a malicious, scandalous, and defamatory newspaper was enjoined. Violation of the court order would result in criminal contempt sanctions. This combination of features led the court to say that as a practical matter the effect of the statute was to require abatement of the existing newspaper and to make further publication punishable as a contempt. "This," said Chief Justice Hughes, "is of the essence of censorship."[18] In the course of his opinion Chief Justice Hughes traced the history of the struggle for freedom of the press and pointed out that freedom from prior restraint was the important issue over which the battle had been fought in England, notably by John Milton. The struggle and protests had been directed against a system whereby no book or publication could be published without submission in advance to the official licensor. If freedom of the press as determined in the American tradition and captured in constitutional provisions can be interpreted by reference to historical considerations, a good case can be made out for the proposition that the freedom of the press referred to in the First Amendment and protected as a 'fundamental liberty under the Due Process Clause is primarily a freedom from prior restraint. It should be added, however, that while the Court has put its emphasis on freedom from prior restraint, most of the cases in which the Court has found state and local legislation invalid because of violation of freedom of the press have been cases dealing with post restraints as previously defined. It may be added that up to this point the Supreme Court has never found any congressional enactment invalid because it abridged freedom of the press. The important cases except for one of the recently decided obscenity cases have arisen under state and local legislation, so that we again have the curious result, assuming that the First Amendment is incorporated in the Fourteenth, that the First Amendment receives its interpretation backhandedly through the interpretation of the Fourteenth.

Validity of and Limitations upon Obscenity Legislation

Against the background of the preceding thumbnail sketch, we turn to the critical problems raised by important decisions of the Supreme Court in recent years dealing with obscenity legislation and movie censorship. Attention will first be directed to the questions raised by national, state, and local legislation designed to deal with the problem of what may be described in a broad way as obscene literature.

Legislation directed against the publication, distribution, and sale of obscene, lascivious, or immoral publications of various kinds is common to all the states. Also, the federal government prohibits the interstate transportation of obscene literature, bars this literature from the mails, and prohibits its importation into the country.[19] A number of states and municipalities in addition may couple with the prohibition on publication of obscene literature a similar prohibition directed against literature which because of its depiction of crimes and violence may have a corrupting effect on the morals of youth.

Does the enforcement of this legislation violate the free press guarantee? Clearly, several types of attacks may be made on this type of legislation depending upon its exact wording and also the means used to enforce it. In the first place, the lack of precise definition of the word "obscene" invites the argument that a criminal statute directed against obscene publications is vague and indefinite and therefore a denial of due process of law. The more fundamental objection, however, is that any restraint on the freedom to publish, distribute, and sell printed materials is a violation of the free press guarantee unless the materials are libelous or serve as an incitement to crime. According to this view, protection of public morality by reference to ideas that may be implanted in minds of persons is not in itself a permissible basis for restricting freedom of the press.

Remedies and methods of enforcement may also raise some special problems. Obviously, a statute that would require a prior approval by a public officer or agency of publications to determine whether they were obscene presents vastly different problems from a statute that punishes publication after the act and only after a judicial hearing of some kind. Does the circulation on an informal basis by a prosecutor or police chief of a memorandum warning booksellers that they will be subject to prosecution unless they remove certain listed books from their shelves operate as a kind of prior restraint which is invalid even though criminal enforcement after publication would be valid? If a proceeding is directed not against a bookseller but against a book for the purpose of determining its obscenity and the court then issues an order banning the further circulation of this book, is this a permissible method for dealing with the problem? Finally, what about a criminal proceeding directed against a bookseller who carries many titles and who can hardly be charged with knowledge of the contents of his books? Is it permissible in a case like this for a state to punish a bookseller without requiring proof of such knowledge with the result that he may be discouraged from selling books as to which and doubt exists? And finally, is it permissible in order to protect the interests of youth to establish prohibitions that apply to the entire population?

Despite the existence of federal and state legislation over a substantial period of time, indeed, going back to the last century, the Supreme Court's definitive decisions on these questions came as a very late development. Undoubtedly, the new and later emphasis on freedom of expression and its relation to the First Amendment has accounted for the Court's readiness in more recent years to subject these problems to closer scrutiny.

Before dealing squarely with the problem of obscenity legislation in the *Roth* and *Alberts* cases in 1957, the Court had already erected some fences for keeping this kind of legislation within limits. In *Winters* v. *New York*[20] the Court had invalidated the New York statute which prohibited the publication of books, comics, etc. which featured crimes of lust and violence on the ground that the statute was so vague and indefinite that it did not serve to give adequate notice of the elements of liability. Then in *Butler* v. *Michigan*[21] the Court invalidated the Michigan statute which prohibited the sale of books tending to corrupt the morals of youth. Without attempting to say what a state could do to protect the morals of youth, the Court did hold that an attempt to solve this problem by prohibiting the sale of books to all people was a case of burning the barn in order to roast the pig. If there was a valid interest to be protected with regard to sales to youth, the statute would have to be more narrowly drafted. In any event the case did establish the principle that freedom to publish literature and to sell the same to the public generally cannot be limited by reference to considerations peculiar to one segment of the population, namely, youth.

Finally, in the *Roth* and *Alberts* cases[22] the Court had before it on consolidated hearing the federal statute making it a crime to send obscene materials in interstate commerce and a California statute punishing the sale and distribution of obscene literature. The Court sustained the convictions under both statutes, but with Justices Black and Douglas dissenting, and with Chief Justice Warren filing a cautious concurring opinion. The gist of Justice Brennan's majority opinion is that obscene publication is not the type of publication that comes within the free press guarantee of the First Amendment since "implicit in the history of the First Amendment is the rejection of obscenity as utterly without redeeming social importance."[23] It is evident that Mr. Justice Brennan makes what we have previously characterized as the definitional or conceptual approach to the problem. The First Amendment protects only certain forms of free press. Obscene publications traditionally do not come within the protected categories. Therefore, a statute punishing the publication of obscene materials is not an abridgment of freedom of the press. It is, of course, clear that this definitional approach is not as simple as it appears, for it is still important to determine in a general way what are the exceptional types of publications denied immunity under the First Amendment and, secondly, what determines the limits of these exceptions. There appears to be as much of a judicial evaluation and appraisal involved in this approach as there is in the familiar judicial approach which either stresses rationality or employs the balance-of-interest technique. This becomes evident when we examine Justice Brennan's opinion to determine what comes within the definition of obscenity. If the historical approach is used to exclude obscene publication from the free press guarantee, then it would seem also that the historical approach would determine the meaning of obscenity. Recourse to history, however, is not completely satisfactory since the crime of obscene libel did not crystallize in English law until after the middle of the last century. But if history is important, then perhaps the famous definition developed by the English courts in *Regina* v. *Hicklin*[24] and later adopted by many American courts would be controlling. According to this case the test to be applied is whether the tendency of the matter charged as being obscene is to deprave and corrupt those whose minds are open to such immoral influences and into whose hands a publication of this sort may fall. Furthermore, in the application of this test it was sufficient to condemn a book as obscene if isolated passages appeared to meet this test. Thus, two factors contributed to make the *Hicklin* test as applied a dragnet for indiscriminate labeling of books as obscene: first, the obscene character of a book was not to be determined by the merit or value of the book as a whole, that is, whether viewed as a whole it had artistic and aesthetic qualities that gave it literary merit, but rather by isolated passages; secondly, the effect of the book as obscene was to be determined by its impact on abnormal or youthful minds rather than on mature adult minds.

Even before the Supreme Court's decision in the *Roth* and *Alberts* cases, the federal courts had rejected the *Hicklin* test and had adopted instead a test that required examination of the book as a whole to determine whether it could properly be classified as a literary work or whether it was dirt for dirt's sake.[25] Some state courts had adopted the same test.[26] One state court had, indeed, gone so far as to say that obscene publication could not be punished unless it presented a clear and present danger of immoral conduct.[27]

What was significant about Justice Brennan's opinion for the Court in the *Roth* and *Alberts* cases was that while placing obscene publication beyond the protection of the First Amendment and declaring such publication to be irrelevant to the free press guarantee, the opinion, nevertheless, stated a constitutional definition that must be observed in the interpretation and application of the federal and state obscenity statutes. The Court defined obscene publications as publications which incite "prurient thought" and stated that the test is "whether to the average person, applying contemporary community standards, the dominant theme of the material taken as a whole appeals to prurient interest."[28] The opinion emphasizes several things in rejecting the *Hicklin* case as an appropriate test of what is constitutionally permissible obscenity legislation. First, obscenity is to be determined by reference to the dominant theme of the whole book. Secondly, a book's obscene character is determined by the impact on the average person. Thirdly, contemporary community standards furnish the yardstick or criterion for determining whether the book can be said to appeal to prurient interest.

The use of the term "prurient" by the Court is no substantial advance on the term "obscene" as generally used and offers no further clue to the meaning of this term. Further clarifying opinions are required in order to make the constitutional standard more precise and meaningful. The Court's decision did, however, serve a useful purpose in clearing the ground of some of the objectionable underbrush associated with the *Hicklin* case. Moreover, the Court's decision may have the effect of spurring state courts into adoption of an even narrower definition of obscenity. Thus, the New York Court of Appeals has recently held that only "hard core pornography" may be reached under the New York statute. The Court of Appeals stated that it is not enough to make a book pornographic that is "aesthetically tasteless and without any redeeming social worth. . . ." Indeed, according to this court a book is not obscene unless it "smacks of sick and blatantly perverse sexuality."[29]

The net result of the *Roth* and *Alberts* decisions is that the federal government and the states may continue to enforce obscenity legislation, provided that the proper test is stated by way of charge to the jury, in the event there is a jury, or otherwise the state court in passing upon the matter observes the proper test as stated in these cases. In the end the question whether a book is obscene is determined by the contemporary moral sense or taste of the community as interpreted by jury or judge.

The Court's later decision in the *Kingsley International Pictures* case[30] bears also on the question of permissible objectives of the state in dealing with what it may regard as objectionable literature. In this case involving the novel *Lady Chatterly's Lover*, the Court held that a New York statute which required denial of a license to motion pictures which are immoral in that they portray "acts of sexual immorality . . . as desirable, acceptable or proper patterns of behavior," and which was construed to forbid the depiction of adultery as an acceptable way of life, did not come within the permissible range of the state's police power. As long as a publication is not obscene and does not incite to illegal conduct, it comes within the range of free expression even though it portrays an unconventional idea. Although this was a film case that arose under a censorship statute, it seems quite clear that the approach made by the Court has an application with respect to all literature and to all restraints on literature whether they be post or prior restraints, namely, that in the interests of protecting public morals a state may not prohibit publications that may portray what by conventional standards are regarded as immoral ideas or an immoral way of life even to the extent of approving the same, so long as it appears in the context of a book or film which is not obscene and which does not incite to unlawful conduct.[31]

The recognition that a state may enforce obscenity legislation still leaves some questions unanswered. May it go beyond enforcement of criminal sanctions and interfere with the free circulation of a book found obscene? Here we get more closely to a question of prior restraint. The issue was raised before

the Court in a case arising under a New York statute pursuant
to which a court, following a judicial determination that a book
was obscene, could enjoin its further circulation and order
copies of the book destroyed. This procedure was held valid.[32]
The important point to observe here is that there was no
general censorship. It was only after the book had been published and copies sold that this proceeding was available.
Indeed, it would appear that if we are to have obscenity
legislation, this is the preferred way of dealing with the problem. Criminal sanctions directed against retail vendors and
distributors are clumsy, ineffective, and likely to work unjust
results. To punish a bookseller because he has held on his
shelves and sold a book which in a criminal proceeding is
shown to be obscene is really to reach the wrong person. If
there is to be any criminal responsibility here it should be
directed against the publisher or author, but this presents
other sticky questions, including questions of jurisdiction. In
any event the uncertainty as to whether a book will be judged
obscene in a judicial proceeding suggests that imposition of
criminal liability is not the appropriate remedy. Indeed, the
Supreme Court has held in a decision following the *Roth* and
Alberts cases that to impose criminal liability on a book dealer
who is innocent of the content and nature of the book is
itself unconstitutional, since it tends to have a harassing and
discouraging effect in respect to the sale of books.[33] The Court
did not completely discount the possibility of criminal prosecution in such a case and suggested that perhaps ways and
means could be found of putting the book dealer on notice.
Certainly, if a book has already been judged obscene in
another jurisdiction and this matter has been called to the
book dealer's attention, he can at that point hardly plead lack
of *scienter* with respect to sales he continues to make.

It may then be suggested that perhaps it would be fairer for a prosecutor or chief of police to distribute to all book dealers within his city or county a list of books regarded as obscene. While this seems to satisfy the requirement of notice and thereby places the book dealer in a better position than otherwise, the system has its own great weakness in that it operates as an informal type of censorship by either a prosecutor or the chief of police and has a harassing effect on the book dealer, who will be inclined to follow the prudent course and keep off his shelves the books on the list. In the end it is the publisher who suffers from this procedure. Whether or not such informal action by prosecutor or police would actually be deemed to constitute an invalid prior restraint is not clear. Several lower court decisions have found this kind of action unconstitutional, and in other cases courts have ordered local authorities to abstain from circulating such a list because of lack of statutory authority.[34] Certainly, the New York procedure whereby a judicial proceeding is initiated against a book is far more satisfactory.

In summary, then, both the federal government and the states may in the exercise of their appropriate spheres of the police power punish the publication, distribution, and sale of obscene books, provided that the *Roth-Alberts* standard or definition of obscenity is observed. Moreover, the sale of books found to be obscene may be enjoined. But a book dealer cannot be punished for the sale of a book unless he can be charged with knowledge of the book's contents.

As long as a Congressional police power in connection with interstate transportation and use of the mails is recognized, there seems to be no reason to deny to Congress the same power the states have unless, as Justice Harlan stated in his opinion in the *Roth* and *Alberts* cases, the distinction is to be observed

between the First Amendment as a limitation on Congress and the Due Process Clause as a limitation on the states. There is much to be said for this thesis and, as previously indicated, the Court needs to resolve in a decisive way the question whether or not the First Amendment is directly applicable to the states and whether and to what extent the restraints in the First Amendment are more restrictive than those embodied in the notion of due process of law. Justice Harlan added further considerations worth noting, namely, that the federal government has only an attenuated interest in this matter and that when it acts to punish or prevent the distribution of literature it has an effect on the whole national scene, as compared with the limited geographical impact of state and local obscenity legislation.

In concluding this discussion it may be observed that despite the dissenting opinions of Justices Black and Douglas in the *Roth* and *Alberts* cases, the power of a state to enact police legislation to protect public morals by means of obscenity laws is far too well supported by history and community opinion to be disregarded by the Court. It must be remembered that obscenity legislation may effect all readers and that it does not operate with discriminatory effect upon one particular group of persons as is the case of legislation directed against expression of political or religious views by unpopular minority groups. Here is a case where the ordinary legislative processes are adequate to deal with the problem and where a preponderant public sentiment should indeed play a controlling part. If people do not care to have obscenity legislation, their efforts should be directed to repeal of this legislation. Obscenity laws may be ill-conceived and inadequate to achieve the purpose of promoting public morals. But it is not the business of the courts to condemn as unconstitutional legislation they may regard as unwise or ineffective.

Censorship of Movies

The problems in respect to obscene literature have centered on the imposition of criminal sanctions after publication and the use of the injunctive process to prevent further sales after a book has been declared obscene in a judicial proceeding. Clearly, the same sanctions applicable to obscene books should be applicable to obscene films, namely, criminal punishment of those who knowingly exhibit obscene films and use of the injunctive process to restrain further exhibition of a film following a judicial determination that it is obscene. The critical problem, however, in regard to movies rises out of censorship arrangements that are prevalent in some states and municipalities whereby every movie must be submitted in advance to a censorship board to determine whether its exhibition is consistent with the standard stated in the statute. A censorship board may find that a movie as a whole violates a standard stated in the statute and therefore deny its approval altogether or it may find that parts of the movie are objectionable and in that case condition its approval on deletion of these parts. The usual censorship statute or ordinance places the authority to view and give approval to films in a board that is not likely to have any special competence in dealing with matters of this kind except as competence of a kind is acquired by experience. This is particularly true of local censorship ordinances that place censorship power in the chief of police or in a certain division of the police department. A censorship board as in the case of the Chicago board may invite private citizens to assist the board in arriving at its judgment.

A review of the Supreme Court's treatment of movies as a form of free press is required before we look more closely at the important recent decision sustaining the principle of movie censorship.

The movies as a form of graphic, pictorial expression did not come into their own until the early part of this century. Today, the movie industry is huge, the movies have become a form of mass entertainment, and the movie as a medium of mass communication has a direct impact and force which give it as some would believe a distinctive quality and characteristic.

Censorship of movies started almost as soon as the movie industry itself became established. Consequently, when dealing with the validity of censorship arrangements, it must be remembered that we are not dealing with anything newly devised but rather with the question of continuing validity of a form of prior restraint that has a substantial history at least in a number of states and municipalities.

When the questions respecting validity of movie censorship first came before the Supreme Court in 1915 in the *Mutual Film Corporation* case,[35] the Supreme Court dismissed the free press aspects of the argument in a rather cavalier way. The Court found that the question of movie censorship raised no substantial question as a restriction on the freedom of the press since theater operators exhibited movies for the purpose of profit and since, so far as the public was concerned, movies were a form of entertainment. It is readily seen that neither of these arguments constitutes a valid ground for denying status to the exhibition of movies as a form of free press and as a fundamental right protected under the liberty clause of the Fourteenth Amendment. It may be said of all book publishers and most newspaper publishers that they are engaged in the business for profit, but this does not in any way impair the fact that they are engaged in the business that involves the freedom of the press. Similarly, the fact that movies may be intended in large part for entertainment should not exclude them from the public press category, since many books and plays and even newspapers in part are devoted to entertainment rather than to education, dissemination of knowledge, and discussion of public issues.

The impact of the *Mutual Film Corporation* case was such that the question of constitutionality of state restrictions on the exhibition of movies was not again considered by the Court until 1952 in the *Joseph Burstyn, Inc.* case.[36] Meanwhile, the movies had assumed a new dimension in American life, and systems of censorship had become well established in some states and municipalities. In the *Burstyn* case the specific question was whether or not the New York Board of Regents, which has authority over movies in that state, lawfully denied permission to show the film *The Miracle* on the ground that it was "sacrilegious" within the meaning of this statute which empowered the board to deny permission if, *inter alia*, a film was found to be sacrilegious. This particular film was objectionable particularly to the Catholic community in the state. The Supreme Court held that the censorship order was invalid since it was based on a ground—namely, sacrilegious—which was too broad and indefinite a standard to serve as a guide to the censor's discretion. Moreover, the state had no legitimate interest in banning the expression of views distasteful to a religious group. The case was equally notable, however, in that the Court for the first time definitely recognized movies as a form of free press and thereby overruled the *Mutual Film Corporation* case.

The *Burstyn* case gave no indication, however, that a majority of the Court were prepared to say that censorship as a form of prior restraint was invalid in itself when applied to the movies. Indeed, Justice Clark's opinion suggested that the Court might take a different view of censorship directed against obscene films. Justice Frankfurter in his separate concurring opinion emphasized the indefiniteness of the standard used. Mr. Justice Reed based his special concurrence on the ground that the film did not seem to be of a character that the First Amendment permitted a state to exclude from public view. Thus, he introduced the idea that the Court's function in review of these cases includes a viewing of the film to determine whether or not the censorship board has acted in a reasonable way in refusing its approval of the film.

It was evident that while the *Burstyn* case established two important principles, namely, that movies were a form of free press and that censorship resting on a vague and indefinite standard was invalid as a restraint on freedom of the press, it still left many questions unanswered. It was not necessary for the Court to deal with the question whether censorship per se was invalid, nor was it necessary for the Court to determine what were either permissible objectives of movie censorship or acceptable statutory standards, nor, except for Justice Reed's opinion, was it clear that the Court was going to undertake and review each film on its merits to determine whether a censorship board's order was arbitrary.

Subsequent developments indicate that the Court was experiencing difficulty in arriving at a definitive position on the question whether censorship per se was invalid and what its function was in review of censorship orders. In a series of subsequent cases the Court did invalidate orders of censorship boards denying approval for the exhibition of films, but in each case this was done by per curiam decision—that is, summary decision without opinion—which cited the *Burstyn*

case and intervening per curiam decisions and left the basic
questions still unresolved. Thus, in *Gelling* v. *Texas*[37] the
Court by per curiam decision invalidated a censorship order
under an ordinance which authorized the board to exclude
films that were prejudicial to the best interests of the people
of the city. Here the reference to the *Burstyn* case in the per
curiam opinion as well as to *Winters* v. *New York* indicated
that the Court thought this was too broad and vague a
standard, and certainly we can all agree with this conclusion.
This was made clear in Justice Frankfurter's concurring opinion. On the other hand Justice Douglas left no doubt in his
separate opinion that he regarded all censorship of movies
as invalid per se since it was a prior restraint on freedom
of press. Thus, by the time the *Gelling* case was decided at
least three possibilities had suggested themselves as to the
Court's treatment of censorship orders: (1) that all censorship of films was invalid; (2) that a censorship order was
invalid if based on a statutory standard that was either
too vague and indefinite or exceeded the proper reach
of the police power; (3) that a censorship order would be
held invalid if the Court on review of the film determined
that there was no basis on which the film could properly be
denied public exhibition. Despite further per curiam decisions
invalidating censorship orders, the basic questions continued
unresolved. Thus, the Court held invalid censorship orders
banning the showing of films where the statute authorized
a board to withhold approval unless in the board's judgment
and discretion the film "was of a moral, educational, amusing
or harmless character,"[38] or if the film was "immoral" and
"tended to corrupt morals,"[39] or if it was "obscene . . . immoral
or tended to debase or corrupt the morals,"[40] or if it was
"immoral and obscene."[41] Although these per curiam decisions

did little to illuminate the Court's basic views on the validity of censorship per se, they did yield some incremental values. Justice Black by this time had aligned himself with Justice Douglas in condemning all censorship as a flagrant prior restraint in violation of the First Amendment. Since in at least some of these cases there had been a private showing of the film for the benefit of the Court as part of the hearing on the validity of the censorship orders, it was evident that some members of the Court were approaching this problem on an *ad hoc* basis.

This was the status of the matter when the Court in 1959 decided the case of *Kingsley International Pictures Corporation v. Regents of the University of the State of New York*.[42] Although this case has already been mentioned in connection with the earlier discussion of obscenity legislation, it merits more extended treatment at this point. The revised New York statute had provided that a license to exhibit a film should issue upon application to the board "unless such film or part thereof is obscene, indecent, immoral, inhuman, sacrilegious, or is of such a character that its exhibition would tend to corrupt morals or incite to crime." A further amendment had provided that "the terms 'immoral' and the phrase 'of such a character that its exhibition would tend to corrupt morals' shall denote a motion picture film or part thereof, the dominant purpose or effect of which is erotic or pornographic; or which portrays acts of sexual immorality, perversion, or lewdness, or which expressly or impliedly presents such acts as desirable, acceptable or proper patterns of behavior." The New York Board of Regents sustained the denial of a license to show the film *Lady Chatterly's Lover* on the ground that the whole theme of the picture was "immoral," since it presented adultery as "a desirable, acceptable, and proper pattern of behavior." The New York Court of Appeals on review of the board's determination sustained the board's action. This was the posture of the case as it reached the Supreme Court. It should be mentioned also that some members of the Supreme Court had viewed the film as part of the review procedure.

The Supreme Court found the censorship order invalid. The chief opinion written by Justice Stewart went beyond a finding that the particular order was invalid and reached the result that the statutory provision as interpreted by the New York Court of Appeals was itself unconstitutional, for it was within the proper sphere of freedom of expression under the First Amendment to depict adultery as a desirable way of life. The majority opinion expressly rejected any theory that the film had been barred because it was obscene or because it was an incitement to unlawful conduct. What made the statute as interpreted by the highest court of the state objectionable was that it barred the portrayal as acceptable behavior of conduct which offended conventional moral standards.

Several opinions in this case brought out the divisions within the Court on the basic problem. Again, Justices Black and Douglas made clear that in their opinion all censorship was invalid. On the other hand, Mr. Justice Frankfurter and Justices Whittaker and Harlan made clear that their objection to the censorship order stemmed from their review of the film which they found to be nonobjectionable and which could not properly be withheld from the public. These three justices asserted that it was an appropriate function for the Court to review each censorship order on its merits. In addition, these three justices disagreed with the majority opinion on the question of whether the statute as such was unconstitutional, since they thought that as properly construed it applied only to films which were obscene or incited to unlawful conduct.

The basic issue successfully avoided in earlier cases was finally and squarely presented to the Court in the recently decided *Times Film* case[43] which arose under the Chicago censorship ordinance. The ordinance authorizes the censoring authority to withhold approval of a film on various grounds, including the ground of obscenity. In this case the movie exhibitor offered to pay the license fee for the showing of a film but refused to submit the film for viewing by the board. Consequently, the censorship authority refused to issue the permit and this order was made final on appeal to the mayor. The sole ground for denial was the petitioner's refusal to submit the film for examination as required by ordinance. The petitioner then brought the suit in the federal district court for an order requiring issuance of the permit without submission of the film and restraining the city officials from interfering with exhibition of the picture.

The case as it came before the Supreme Court then raised only the issue whether a statute or ordinance requiring a censorship board's advance approval for the showing of a film is in itself unconstitutional, quite apart from the grounds on which approval of a film can be denied and quite apart from the merits of the censorship board's action in dealing with a particular film. The exhibitor here made no attempt to get the board's approval and there is nothing to indicate that approval of this film would have been withheld if application had been made. From the viewpoint of constitutional arguments, the exhibitor gambled by putting all his eggs in one basket.

Faced with the question of validity of censorship per se, the Court held that the Chicago ordinance was not invalid on its face. In short, movie censorship is not unconstitutional per se. This decision thus puts to rest a question on which a majority of the Court had not previously taken a position. The chief opinion by Mr. Justice Clark is a relatively brief one. After pointing out that the Court had not previously passed upon the validity of prior restraint in regard to movies, and that even Chief Justice Hughes in *Near* v. *Minnesota*[44] had indicated by way of dictum that prior restraint might be permissible in some circumstances, the Court stated that the issue was whether or not the movie exhibitor had a right to exhibit, at least once, any and every kind of motion picture. The Court denied this right and, pointing to its decisions upholding the validity of legislation dealing with obscene publications, it stated that Illinois was not to be denied what it might consider to be the most effective remedy dealing with the problem of showing obscene films. Furthermore, the Court made mention of the arguments of earlier cases that certain types of expression do not come within' the freedom of the press idea. If, as the Court had held in the *Roth* and *Alberts* cases, obscene publication does not come under the First Amendment's protection, then the case against prior restraint is weaker, although not completely irrelevant. Perhaps the nub of Justice Clark's opinion is found in his statement: "It is not for this Court to limit the state in its selection of the remedy it deems most effective to cope with such a problem, absent, of course, a showing of unreasonable strictures on individual liberty resulting from its application in particular circumstances."[45] It is evident from the majority opinion that the Court's thinking was centered on the municipality's power to deal with obscene films. If there is a power to protect the public against the evils of obscene films, then it is not for the Court to dictate to the legislative authorities the appropriate means of dealing with the problem.

Four members of the Court dissented. The chief dissenting opinion was written by Chief Justice Warren, and joined by Justices Black, Douglas, and Brennan. This long dissenting opinion develops the thesis first of all that the Court has over a period of years shown an opposition to all forms of prior restraint and that any prior restraint is in itself an invalid restriction on freedom of the press protected under the First and Fourteenth amendments. In reaching this point the Court puts into a single bundle all the types of cases involving prior restraints and refuses to consider the problem in regard to censorship of movies as standing in a special category. Thus, the Court includes decisions such as *Lovell* v. *Griffin*,[46] where there were no grounds at all stated for guiding the police chief's discretion in deciding whether to grant or withhold a permit to distribute literature. In any event the Chief Justice distills from prior cases and expressions of opinion a general principle that all prior restraint is invalid. Declaring that he sees no reason and no constitutional principle that would justify treating movies in a separate category, the Chief Justice concludes that if censorship is valid in regard to movies there is no reason why it cannot be extended to all the other forms of expression. The Chief Justice then illustrates by a series of specific instances how censorship boards do their work and in how arbitrary a way they carry on, often at the expense of denying the public the opportunity to view films and parts of films that have an important bearing on current economic, political, and social problems. This part of the Chief Justice's dissent is impressive in showing the dangers of abuse that results from any system of censorship. The dissenting opinion goes on to state that there is an important difference between prior restraint and post restraint and that a criminal prosecution would not be undertaken except after a prosecutor has carefully studied the matter and that even then the matter comes for adjudication before a court. Chief Justice Warren says that the majority opinion does not correctly state the issue when it says that the question is whether an exhibitor has a right under any circumstance to show a film at least once. He says the issue is rather whether or not the barring of a film can be effectuated without showing that a film's exhibition will impair some vital public interest. The Chief Justice's opinion at this point seems to be circular. In the first place, the exhibitor did not challenge the statutory grounds on which films could be denied, and obviously the censorship board had no way in which to determine whether or not the movie violated a statutory standard unless it first had an opportunity to see it.

Justice Black, in a dissenting opinion concurred in by Chief Justice Warren and Justice Douglas, affirmed his earlier position that all censorship is unconstitutional.

In review of and comment on this case, it should be made clear that the Court in reaching the result it did was not departing from any controlling precedent. Indeed, the whole history of the cases dealing with movie censorship made clear that a majority of the Court had left the question open. Nor did other cases dealing with other phases of freedom of expression establish a general and immutable principle of freedom from prior restraint. The cases involving licensing requirements for persons distributing literature on sidewalks and making use of public parks all turned on the grant of unlimited discretionary power or failure to employ definite standards. Indeed, there is not a single case in the history of our constitutional litigation where the Court was called upon to consider the validity of a statute which requires advance approval of a publication by a board operating within the limits of a statute directed toward permissible police power ends and employing a standard which is recognized as appropriate for this purpose.

It is, nevertheless, true that the Court has repeatedly said that freedom from prior restraint is the most important feature of freedom of the press, and certainly history supports this conclusion.

Undoubtedly the sympathies and predilections of many people are attracted to the dissenting opinion which strikes a bold note in favor of freedom from all forms of prior restraint even where the purpose may be directed to prevent the circulation of obscene materials. We may be sure that the judges constituting the majority in the *Times Film* case have no personal predilections in favor of film censorship whether at Chicago or elsewhere. Indeed, we may well suppose that they regard such censorship as unwise and undesirable. For them, however, the question was one of appropriate exercise of judicial power in determining what limitations are placed upon the states under the Fourteenth Amendment. This case presents in critical focus the question whether the states on issues of this kind are limited by the Due Process Clause or by the First Amendment. Justice Clark for the majority speaks of the Fourteenth and First amendments, but it seems to me that the analysis by the Court of the problem and the judicial technique employed by it is a technique that is characteristic of the usual treatment of the due process problem where substantive liberties are involved, namely, whether the city in this case has acted unreasonably or arbitrarily in subjecting the movie exhibitor to this restraint on his liberty. In emphasizing the power of the state of Illinois through its municipality to determine the most effective remedy for combating evils which the legislature anticipated in regard to the exhibition of obscene films and in conceding the power of a legislature to classify movies separately for the purpose of restraint, the Court engaged in the kind of judicial toleration of state legislative policy which is characteristic of the due process cases and bears the imprint of Justice Holmes's approach in terms of the reasonable man. In short, the opinion evidences a reluctance on the part of the majority to substitute their own views for that of the legislature in determining appropriate policy objectives and the means of achieving them. This is a legitimate interpretation of due process of law in its application to substantive freedoms. On the other hand, the dissenting opinion proceeds on a premise and on an assumption as to the propriety of judicial review which is associated with the ideas that have clustered around the First Amendment, namely, that these freedoms are preferred and that no intrusions will be permitted unless demanded by public necessity, and that the need for this kind of restriction will be more closely inquired into than in the ordinary case of due process considerations. The majority opinion in substance conforms to the idea expressed by Justice Harlan in his separate opinion in the obscenity cases, where he drew a clear distinction between the First Amendment as a restriction on Congress and the Fourteenth Amendment as a restriction on the states. Thus, while the *Times Film* case spoke of the First Amendment, the methodology is that of due process.[47]

As to the statement in the dissenting opinion that if censorship is permitted in regard to movies there is no constitutional principle that would prevent its extension to other forms of expression including newspapers and books, it may be enough to say, first of all, that the Court is competent to fashion constitutional principles by reference to problems peculiar to a given category of cases. Unless the Court is ready to concede there is no difference between a mass medium of expression such as the movies and other forms of expression such as newspapers and books, it is hard to understand why consistent with this case the Court could not invalidate any prior restraints made applicable in regard to books and newspapers. Moreover, as a practical matter the case reduces itself to the proposition that advance approval of a film may be required for the limited purpose of determining whether a film is obscene. At least the Court has not up to this point indicated a willingness to tolerate any other standard for this purpose.[47a]

It is useful, perhaps, to note that the four judges who dissented here dissented also in an earlier case on the question whether the sale of a book could be stopped and its destruction ordered once the book was found to be obscene.[48] Three of the dissenting justices[49] appear to be opposed to any kind of prior restraint on the free circulation of books or exhibition of films even if found to be obscene in a judicial proceeding. On the other hand, the argument was made that while a film can be enjoined after it is found to be obscene by a court, at least it is entitled to one public showing. The application of this idea to films is not altogether clear. If, for instance, a film could be shown once in Chicago and then a temporary injunction secured and this injunction made final after a judicial hearing, a question may be raised as to the substantiality of the distinction between this procedure and the kind of censorship practiced in Chicago. The only difference that has practical significance is that in the one case there is a judicial hearing rather than a hearing by an administrative body.

Several points may be noted in concluding this discussion of film censorship. First of all, the Court's readiness to tolerate

advance censorship makes it all the more important that the
Court see to it that this kind of censorship, which is not simply
concerned with what may be shown to children but shown to
the adult community as well, be limited to the single purpose
of determining whether a film is obscene and that the Court
apply a strict standard for this purpose. Although the term
"obscenity" as defined by the Court in *Roth* may be adequate
for the purpose of post-publication restraints, it does not follow
that the Court should not define the term more narrowly and
precisely for purpose of advance censorship, so as to include
only clearly pornographic pictorial presentation.[50] The Court
should also insist that censorship boards follow a procedure
that requires them to put their findings on record so as to
lay a foundation for judicial review in order to determine
whether the board has applied the proper standard and whether
it has taken irrelevant considerations into account. Finally,
the Court must necessarily reserve to itself and exercise the
authority to review the merits of a censorship order in a specific
case in order to make certain that the film merits the action
taken by the board. Obviously, this imposes a much larger
task on the Court than if it had followed the simpler expedient
of declaring all censorship invalid. To be sure this encounters
the objection made by Justice Black that a review by the Court
of the merits of each film makes the Court a board of censors
and that it is no more equipped to do this than any other board
of censors. But to deny that it is an appropriate judicial function to determine whether a given publication is obscene is to
deny the validity of all obscenity legislation itself. The majority
of the Court in the *Roth* and *Alberts* cases conceded that
obscenity legislation was valid and stated the importance of
proper definition and standard. The court that has elaborated

the definition of obscenity is in the best position to determine its meaning by reference to a given case.

Recognizing that the police power may be exercised to protect the public morals, the Court has sanctioned obscenity legislation and advance film censorship. It does not follow that legislation of this kind, if it goes beyond the problem of dealing with blatant pornography, is effective to serve its intended ends or that any public good achieved from it counterbalances the risks entailed in restricting freedom of expression. The law is powerless to improve the public taste. As long as the public shows an interest in books, magazines, and films that deal with life in a cheap, tawdry, and degrading way, we shall continue to have literature and films published to cater to this taste. So far as the morals of children and youth are concerned, the primary responsibility rests on the home, the school, and the church for more effective leadership in guiding the tastes and habits of children, and any legislation oriented to this end should, as far as practicable, deal narrowly and specifically with the problem in respect to minors rather than operate as a broadside restriction on the reading and viewing tastes of the entire adult community.

III. FREEDOM OF ASSOCIATION
AND FREEDOM FROM DISCLOSURE:
THE BALANCING OF INTERESTS

Included among the important decisions handed down by the Supreme Court during the 1960 term were five decisions that serve very adequately as a basis for this chapter. Although an *ad hoc* presentation and examination of a series of cases are not always either interesting or profitable, at least a summary look at these five cases is worth our attention at the outset both because of the interest attaching to the problems with which these cases dealt and because they do serve in such an effective way to pinpoint the questions and policies I propose to discuss.

Five Recent Decisions by the Supreme Court

1. *Communist Party of the United States v. Subversive Activities Control Board.*[1] In this case the Court held valid the provision of the Internal Security Act of 1950 requiring the so-called Communist-action organizations to register and to furnish a list of their officers and members. It further upheld the determination by the Subversive Activities Control Board, on the basis of extended hearings and a formidable record developed in a proceeding that began in 1950, that the Communist Party is a Communist-action organization within the meaning of the statute in that it is controlled by a foreign government and has as its objectives the furtherance

of a world-wide revolutionary movement whose purpose it is, by treachery, deceit, infiltration into other groups, espionage, sabotage, terrorism, and any other means deemed necessary, to establish a Communist totalitarian dictatorship in the countries throughout the world through the medium of a world-wide Communist organization. The effect of the Court's decision is that the Communist Party through its officers is now required to file a registration statement including a list of its members.[2] Failure to register as required is made a punishable offense. Moreover, in the case of an organization which is registered or is required to register, other sanctions become applicable. Thus certain acts of the Party by way of distribution of publications through the mails or through the instrumentalities of interstate or foreign commerce, or causing matter to be broadcast by radio or television, are prohibited unless any such publication is labeled as a publication by the Communist Party. Tax exemption is denied to an organization found to be a Communist-action organization. Members of such an organization are forbidden to apply for or use a United States passport, to hold government or defense facility employment, or to hold office in a labor union. Members of such an organization may be deported, may not be naturalized, and may in some circumstances be denaturalized. The Court in its recent decision found it unnecessary to pass on the validity of these additional sanctions since no present controversy was raised in respect to them. Likewise, the majority, speaking through Mr. Justice Frankfurter, stated that it was premature to consider the important issue of self-incrimination raised under the Fifth Amendment in the event a registration statement is filed. This presents a very real issue since a disclosure of names of officers and members would aid the government in prosecution under the Smith

Act. It is evident that the last word has not yet been said on this problem.

On the constitutional issue that the requirement of registration of the Party violated the First Amendment, the Court held that the duty to register and to disclose the required information did not violate the freedoms of speech, press, and association since, in view of the nature of the organization and its objectives, Congress could properly determine that these requirements were essential in order to protect important public interests. The Court found ample precedent in the laws requiring registration of agents of foreign governments and registration by lobbyists.

Four justices dissented. Justices Brennan and Douglas while agreeing that the registration requirement was in itself constitutional dissented on the ground that compulsory disclosure of names of officers and members violated the Fifth Amendment—an issue which they thought appropriately raised at this time. Chief Justice Warren, who dissented on statutory and evidentiary grounds, thought that it was premature to pass on any constitutional issues, but since the other members of the Court had reached the constitutional questions, he concurred in Justice Brennan's opinion on these questions. Justice Black, while dissenting on other grounds also, pitched his dissent primarily on the ground that the legislation was directed to the ultimate purpose of imposing sanctions and disabilities on persons because they were members of the Communist Party and so viewed it violated freedom of speech and association under the First Amendment.

On the primary issue before the Court, seven members of the Court were agreed that a requirement that the Communist Party register as a Communist-action organization was not in itself unconstitutional. At this point it is worth emphasizing that a substantial majority of the Court found no error in the determination by the Subversive Activities Control Board that the Communist Party is an organization controlled by a foreign government and that it has as its objective the furtherance of the world-wide Communist conspiracy and aims at installation of "a Soviet style dictatorship in the United States."

2. *Scales v. United States.*[3] Here the Court, speaking through Justice Harlan, upheld the conviction of Scales under the provision of the Smith Act making it a crime for a person knowingly to be a member of an organization which advocates the overthrow of government by force. Overcoming a number of statutory difficulties the Court held that the statute in punishing knowing membership should be construed to mean membership that was active and which was purposive in the sense that the member was identified with organizational activities that constituted an incitement to future overthrow of the government by violence if necessary in order to achieve the organization's objectives. Reviewing the record in the case, the Court determined that Scales had actively engaged in a program of the Communist Party which was an incitement to action by way of violent overthrow of government and more than a teaching or advocating of violent overthrow as an abstract doctrine. The Court thus related the knowing membership clause to the provisions of the Smith Act punishing conspiracy to advocate overthrow by force and which as construed in the *Dennis* and *Yates* cases[4] was held constitutionally applicable to concerted activities of Communist Party members found to constitute an incitement to action directed at forcible overthrow of government, that is, aimed at building up a seditious group and maintaining it in readiness for action at a propitious time. Recognizing that the statute

distinguished between knowing membership in a party that advocated forcible overthrow of government and criminal liability based on a conspiracy charge, the Court stated that, nevertheless, there was a striking similarity between holding a person liable on a charge of conspiracy directed to criminal objectives and an active and purposive membership in a party which is found by reference to the evidence before the Court to be engaging in activities that constitute incitement to acts of forcible overthrow of government. The Court rejected the argument that the statute was invalid on the due process ground that it established guilt by association, since the statute did not punish membership as such.

Again four justices dissented. Justice Brennan, joined by Chief Justice Warren, dissented on the ground that a provision of the Internal Security Act was intended to immunize Communist Party membership from liability under the knowing membership clause of the Smith Act. Justice Douglas, while agreeing on this point, dissented on the further grounds that the statute created guilt by association and violated the First Amendment by restricting the free expression of political ideas and freedom of political association. Pointing to the right of revolution recognized in American history and in the specific provisions of a number of state constitutions, he defended the right of persons and parties to advocate radical ideas, even overthrow of government by force, so long as this advocacy does not assume the form of revolution or actual incitement to revolution. Justice Black, while agreeing with other dissenters, expressed the further objection that defendants were found guilty of a crime of which they were not charged and also took occasion again to criticize the balance-of-interest technique whereby the Court in his opinion is devitalizing the First Amendment freedoms.

3. *Wilkinson* v. *United States.*[5] Here the Court upheld the defendant's conviction under the federal statute making it a crime to willfully refuse to answer a pertinent question put by a Congressional committee. Wilkinson refused to answer the question whether he was a Communist in the course of a committee investigation of Communist infiltration into textile industries in the South and the related question of Communist propaganda in the South. He defended his refusal on the grounds, among others, that the First Amendment assured him privacy with respect to his political belief and association. Relying on the earlier *Barenblatt* case,[6] the majority held that Wilkinson's First Amendment interest in nondisclosure was outweighed by the national interest in requiring disclosure of Communist affiliation pursuant to its power to investigate subversive activities in their relation to the national security. Chief Justice Warren and Justices Black, Douglas, and Brennan dissented on the ground that the real purpose here in questioning Wilkinson was not to elicit information needed about Communism but to harass and expose a man who had criticized the committee's work and encouraged opposition to it.

4. *Konigsberg* v. *State Bar of California.*[7] Konigsberg, a California citizen, who had passed the state bar examination, was required to demonstrate his character and fitness to practice law, including a showing that he was a person of good moral character and did not advocate overthrow of government by force. An impressive array of testimony by friends, neighbors, and public-minded citizens supported the conclusion that he was a person of good character and loyal to his country. Moreover, he testified that he did not and never had advocated the overthrow of government by force. Nevertheless, because of some of his publications and public utterances, he was asked

by the committee whether he was a member of the Communist Party. He refused to answer this question, denying its relevancy and claiming that examination into this matter violated rights reserved under the First and Fourteenth amendments. Because of his refusal to answer this question, the bar examiners refused to approve his admission to the bar. This action was affirmed by the state supreme court. On review the United States Supreme Court held that the question whether Konigsberg was a Communist was relevant to an inquiry into fitness to practice law and that, while this inquiry did intrude into the area of First Amendment freedoms, any right to silence here was counterbalanced by an appropriate state interest.[8] It should be emphasized that the Court did not say that disclosure of Communist affiliation would be a basis for denying admission but held only that the committee was constitutionally entitled to make the inquiry and to require the disclosure. Again the Warren-Black-Douglas-Brennan bloc dissented on the ground that the Board was not really interested in determining Konigsberg's fitness since this had already been demonstrated, but rather was intent on exposing him by an inquiry that extended into the sheltered area of the First Amendment.

5. *Louisiana* v. *NAACP*.[9] A Louisiana statute made it unlawful for any nontrading association affiliated with an out-of-state association to do business in the state unless it filed an affidavit that officers of the affiliated association were not members of the Communist Party or any other subversive organization. A second statute required every nonprofit organization to file an annual registration statement giving a complete list of its officers and members. In this case the Supreme Court held that any attempt to enforce these statutes against

the NAACP by denying it a right to carry on its activities in Louisiana unless these requirements were satisfied violated the freedom of association protected under the Fourteenth and First amendments. The Court accepted the finding below that compliance with the first statute was impossible, as a practical matter, and that filing a list of members under the second statute would result in community reprisals and sanctions against these persons. In basing its case on freedom of association as a distinct right, the Court relied on recent cases where this right was first recognized by the Court.

This case involving the NAACP furnishes an interesting and dramatic contrast to the cases dealing with the matter of Communist affiliation. According to the cases, Congress may require a disclosure of Communist affiliation by requiring the Communist Party to register itself and to furnish a list of its members, and persons called before Congressional investigating committees investigating subversive activities may properly be required to disclose Communist affiliation. Moreover, participation in the affairs of the Communist Party may properly result in a conviction on a charge of conspiracy to advocate overthrow of government by force, and active and purposive membership in the Communist Party may itself give rise to criminal liability. Likewise, the question of Communist affiliation may properly be inquired into as a condition of admission to the state bar, and, as other cases demonstrate,[10] as a condition of public employment. Likewise, loyalty oaths disclaiming membership in organizations that advocate overthrow of government by force have been upheld.[11]

On the other hand, a state cannot require the NAACP as a condition of doing business in the state to disclose its membership list because of the fear of sanctions and reprisals against the members. Here the association is really asserting rights on behalf of its members in refusing the state's demand. Likewise, any general requirement that a person disclose his affiliation as to membership organizations is unconstitutional.[12] What then is the difference between statutes and governmental actions requiring disclosure of Communist affiliation that have been upheld and statutes requiring disclosure of NAACP affiliation that have been held invalid? The answer is not difficult to find. In view of the identification of the Communist Party with purposes related to forcible overthrow of government, an unlawful objective, it is appropriate to require identification of persons as Communists and disclosure of Communist activity as well as to punish under criminal legislation those in any way actively engaged in this program. On the other hand, the purposes of the NAACP are not directed toward unlawful ends. It is not a political party. It is a nonprofit association directed to the advancement of the interests of its members and of the Negro race generally. None of its objectives can be regarded as invalid under federal or state law. This appears to be the whole distinction. In this connection we may also consider the Court's decision rendered some years ago when it upheld a New York statute which was aimed at the purpose of requiring a registration by the Ku Klux Klan and a disclosure by it of its membership list. The Court held this to be a valid exercise of the state's police power.[13] If there is to be any difference noted between the state's power to compel disclosure by the Ku Klux Klan, on the one hand, and the NAACP, on the other, it must be on some ground disclosed by a record that the Ku Klux Klan was known at the time to engage in unlawful activities.

Freedom of Association and of Nondisclosure

The cases involving the Communist Party, on the one hand, and the NAACP, on the other, involve two common problems referred to in the title of this chapter, namely, the right of association and the related freedom of nondisclosure in regard to association membership. We should like to say a further word about these matters and particularly the right of association. Just what is meant by this right, what is its constitutional source, and what is its significance?

When we speak of freedom of association we may have reference to it in a variety of contexts. Probably the highest form of freedom of association, at least as many would see it, is the freedom to associate for political purposes by means of organization of a political party and participation in its activities. The effective functioning of a democratic society depends on the formation of political parties and the use of parties as vehicles for the formulation and expression of opinions and policies. The minority party or parties become vehicles for registering opposition and dissent. The political party is the indispensable agency both for effective participation in political affairs by the individual citizen and for registering the diversity of views in a pluralistic society. Indeed, under some other constitutional systems political parties are viewed as organs of government and have a high constitutional status.

The idea that has recently been stressed in the Supreme Court's decisions that there is a freedom of association has not been developed in the context of the political party issue, however, but rather by reference to organizations that are not political parties but which are organized as nonprofit associations or groups and designed to serve perhaps any number of purposes in regard to advancement of the interests of members of the organization or a larger constituency served by it. The NAACP, of course, furnishes the best illustration of this. It is not a political party; it does not operate for profit; it is, as its own statement of purpose indicates, an organization devoted to promoting the welfare of the Negro in the United States. Its position has come to the fore in recent years because of its vigorous and aggressive espousal of the legal rights of Negroes, and it in substance has been carrying a large part of the load with respect to litigation designed to secure enforcement of the Supreme Court's desegregation decree and also in other cases involving equal protection claims. Because of its identification with these programs, the organization naturally has fallen into disfavor in a number of communities. The organization and its members are viewed as agitators and, indeed, there is the tendency, as is so often the case these days, to identify any group or organization that is ready to promote changes that interfere with the *status quo* as a radical or subversive organization. It is because of the efforts to throttle the NAACP under various laws requiring registration, payment of license taxes, and filing of data and information including membership lists that the Court has really had occasion to inquire into the nature of a nonprofit association and its constitutional rights and even more importantly the rights of its members to associate together to achieve common objectives.

The right of association as a distinctive, substantive freedom was first enunciated by the Supreme Court in *NAACP v. Alabama*,[14] where the Court held that Alabama could not require the NAACP, in connection with any duty it had, to comply with a statute with respect to doing local business, to disclose its membership list, since it appeared under the circumstances that this disclosure would be used as a means of subjecting the members to community sanctions and reprisals. This case involved a state statute and the Court found that the statute, which as interpreted required a disclosure of membership lists, operated to deprive the association's members of their liberty without due process of law. Justice Harlan stated that the right to form an association for the advancement of ideas was indisputably a part of the liberty protected by the Due Process Clause. Alabama stated no valid interest here in requiring disclosure of members even though the state could to some extent regulate the doing of business by the association. Then in *Bates* v. *City of Little Rock*[15] the Court built further on the idea by holding invalid in its application to the NAACP a municipal ordinance requiring all organizations doing business locally to pay a license tax and file a registration statement which included a list of members. Again, the disclosure of membership was not seen to be relevant to the municipality's interest in regulating and taxing nonprofit associations.

The recent case of *Shelton* v. *Tucker*,[16] arising under an Arkansas statute, goes even further in that it holds that a state may not require public employees—in this case school teachers—to furnish as a condition of employment a list of all membership activities or a list of all organizations to which they made contributions. The Court here did not rest its case on a finding that this was motivated by a purpose of requiring disclosure of NAACP affiliation, although this might well have been the case, but on the broader basis that there is a right of privacy in regard to a person's organizational activities, and that whatever power a state has to compel disclosure of its employees in regard to legitimate public interests cannot justify a statute as sweeping in its character as this statute—

one which would require a person to disclose not only affiliation with organizations designed to influence public opinion and participate in the political process or to improve the status of the members but affiliation also with church organizations and the like. In other words the statute was much too broad. The Court's opinion does suggest that a more narrowly drafted statute might properly serve the state's aim. A school board may have an interest in inquiring into its teachers' outside activities in order to see to what extent teachers are spending their time on outside organizational work. But certainly any such limited and modest interest the state may properly assert would be satisfied by a much less sweeping requirement than that a complete disclosure be made of all organizations to which a member belongs or which he supports.

The recently developed right of association has its chief significance as an independent right in respect to an organization that is aimed at improvement of conditions or advancement of the interests of the members of the organization, but not identifiable as a political party. This freedom of association emerges as a fundamental right protected under the Due Process Clause. It is apparent, of course, that some of these nonprofit associations do engage in activities that involve free speech, free press, and even freedom of assembly, as distinguished from organizations that are strictly social organizations in the sense that persons belong to them in order to enjoy the social amenities and enjoy an opportunity for fraternization, although certainly the right of association should extend to these as well.

There is, of course, another right of association directed to strictly economic ends. This includes the right of persons to form a labor union as a means of advancing their interests and, on the other hand, the rights of employers or businessmen to join a trade association to promote their common interests. And there is the right of association, if we may speak of it, on the part of persons to work together in a common effort such as in a partnership or in an unincorporated joint venture or association. Finally, of course, we must mention at this point the use of the corporate device as a means of association for the purpose of pooling capital, engaging in a common enterprise, and avoiding the risks of individual or noncorporate enterprise. We may isolate the trade union and the business corporation and association from the problem under discussion since their activities are primarily economic in character, although I should add that it is now recognized that the right to form and carry on the activities of a labor union is a fundamental right under the national labor relations legislation.[17] There is no right on the part of persons to organize a corporate body to carry on business, this being a matter of dispensation by the state. On the other hand, the activities of labor unions and trade associations should not be too sharply distinguished in terms of freedom of speech and freedom of the press since many of their activities are related to support of public policies and advocacy of ideas that play a legitimate part in the determination of legislative policy. Indeed, the Supreme Court has recognized that efforts by both union and corporate bodies to influence public opinion and legislative policy are an appropriate expression of free speech, subject to the legislative power to prescribe restrictions designed to protect public and private interests.[18]

The question may be asked at this point, just what is embraced by the right of association as a fundamental liberty embraced by the Due Process Clause? Certainly, it embraces the right to join with others in an association to pursue common ends—social, political, and economic. It includes the right of a strictly private association to determine its own membership and to establish rules and regulations governing the conduct of its members. It includes the right of the association to carry on its activities subject to restrictions reasonably imposed in the exercise of its police powers to protect appropriate public interests. To what extent an unincorporated association—whether a social club, a philanthropic association, or a nonprofit organization dedicated to altruistic or social betterment purposes, but not engaged in business in the usual sense and not claiming special tax privileges for itself—can be required to register or to pay privilege taxes on its activities, are questions that remain to be answered. In any event it is clear that the organization cannot be required to disclose its membership list under circumstances that subject its members to the risk of nonlegal disabilities or sanctions, and in turn any sweeping requirement by law that a person make a disclosure of membership in nonprofit associations is equally invalid. Moreover, the close identity between the association and its members makes it appropriate for the association in a legal proceeding to raise objections that go to the rights of its members.

Freedom of Nonassociation

Although it diverts somewhat from the main line of this discussion, the further question may be raised whether there is in turn a constitutional right of freedom from association. Does a person have a right not to join? No one would hesitate to give an affirmative answer to this question stated in the abstract. A person should be allowed to pick his associates, the organizations he belongs to, and the causes he wishes to support. The question really becomes relevant, however, only in the context of the kinds of problems that came before the Supreme Court during the past term. Does an employee have a right to work free from compulsory union membership in a closed shop, where the closed shop is sanctioned by law as under federal labor legislation? And does an attorney have a right to be free from compulsory membership in the organized bar pursuant to an integrated bar arrangement? These questions become concrete as they affect the pocketbook because of the duty to pay dues. In these cases the compulsory association in terms of duty to support the association by payment of dues is related to the pursuit of one's work and the practice of one's profession. The Court's decisions this past term,[19] whatever else they may mean, sustained legislation authorizing closed shop agreements and a state integrated bar arrangement on the theory that they serve valid, common, and public interests that override individual objections. The really critical question raised in these cases, however, goes to a more important question: may a person be required by law to pay dues to a labor union that carries on political activities that are objectionable to him, and may an attorney be required to pay dues to an integrated bar that supports legislative programs offensive to him? The Constitution assures freedom of speech, press, and assembly and the cognate freedom of political association, as well as the right to vote in accordance with the dictates of one's conscience. These freedoms by implication assure the individual's freedom not to be coerced into supporting political candidates not of his own choosing or legislation which he personally opposes. Does this mean then that a labor union which is party to a closed shop arrangement may not use any part of funds collected from dues to engage in political activities and that an integrated

bar may not use dues to support legislative proposals? The
Court's recent decisions give no clear-cut answer to these
questions. In the closed shop case the majority held, as a
matter of interpretation of federal railway labor legislation,
that a union could not use any part of an objecting employee's dues to support political activities,[20] and in the integrated bar case the chief opinion held that the parallel
question whether an attorney could object on constitutional
grounds to the use of any part of his dues to support legislation
he opposes was not properly before the Court at this time.[21]
In short, these decisions leave the basic constitutional issue
unsettled.

Freedom of Political Association and the First Amendment

We return now to the main theme respecting freedom
of association and freedom of nondisclosure of association
membership as developed in the cases dealing with the
NAACP and shall pursue further the questions raised in
regard to the Court's totally different treatment of these
questions as they relate to the Communist Party. I suggested
earlier that freedom of political association, exercised in the
organization of a political party and participation in its
activities, may be regarded as the highest form of association
since it directly involves the First Amendment freedoms and
the central and distinguishing aspects of a democratic society.
Yet the Court has sanctioned severe restrictions on the Communist Party that are not tolerated in respect to the NAACP,
and I am sure would not be tolerated in regard to other political
parties. The Communist Party may be required to register
under the Internal Security Act,[22] witnesses before Congressional committees investigating Communist propaganda

and penetration of Communists into vital areas of American life may be forced to disclose Communist affiliation where this question is relevant by reference to what the committee already knows about the witness,[23] persons seeking public employment or admission to a quasi-public profession like the bar may be required to disclose Communist affiliation,[24] concerted activities by Communists supporting a finding of incitement to forcible overthrow of government warrant conviction under the Smith Act,[25] and, indeed, membership in the Party, if active and purposive in respect to advocacy of forcible overthrow, is in itself punishable.[26]

The central reason in justification for this drastic treatment of one political party and its members is clear. The Communist Party is not just a minority political party operating within the framework of a democratic structure and committed to political and economic change by peaceful parliamentary means. Already in the *Douds* case,[27] where the Court upheld the non-Communist affidavit requirement of the National Labor Relations Act, Justice Jackson pointed out that Congress had before it adequate evidence to support a Congressional finding that the Party was distinctive from other political parties in numerous important respects. Certainly, the finding of the Subversive Activities Control Board made after extended hearings and study, and supported by the Supreme Court's recent decision,[28] that the Communist Party is an organization controlled by a foreign government and pursuing objectives that identify it with a world-wide Communist conspiracy aimed, *inter alia,* at the establishment of a Soviet-type totalitarian dictatorship in the United States, should put this question beyond doubt.

This finding, however, does not answer all constitutional questions raised in respect to the total mass of the internal security program. Whether the well-documented conclusion that the Communist Party is controlled by a foreign government and is part of a total conspiracy directed to revolutionary objectives supports criminal sedition prosecutions under the Smith Act, whether it is a justification for compelling witnesses to disclose Communist affiliation before a Congressional committee, or as a condition to public or quasi-public employment, raises the issues on which the Court has been so sharply divided. But before we note the differences within the Court, it will be well to emphasize the points of substantial agreement.

The recent decision holding valid the registration requirement of the Internal Security Act, subject to further determination of the self-incrimination question—itself a vital phase of the nondisclosure problem—is highly significant since a substantial majority of the Court are agreed that findings support the conclusion that the Communist Party is so totally different from other American political parties as to require registration. Likewise, there is no doubt that a substantial majority of the Court regard it as an appropriate function for Congress through an investigating committee to study Communism and the Communist Party and to expose the Party's effort to develop its objectives by propaganda and by penetration into vital phases of American life, such as labor unions, education, and even churches. Exposure of the Party's objectives and techniques is appropriate to the legislative function, both because it may demonstrate the need for new or revised legislation and because it lays a foundation for educating the American people on the nature of the Communist conspiracy.

It is fair to say also that there is no disagreement on the bench on the proposition that there is a right to criticize the government, to dissent from existing legislative policies and programs, to criticize democracy, capitalism, free enterprise, the Constitution, and whatever may be meant by the American way of life, to be a thorough nonconformist and to be completely unorthodox with respect to American patterns of political, economic, and social life, to espouse radical political and economic change, to support proposals for abolishing the Constitution and establishing a Communist dictatorship, indeed, to teach the right and propriety of revolution as a means of achieving change provided this is abstract and academic and unrelated to an action program. And, on the other hand, the Court would all agree that Congress has a broad power to act to protect the national security, to punish revolutionary acts, to punish sabotage, espionage, incitement to criminal conduct, and conspiracy to overthrow the government.

A vital point of disagreement is at what point speech activities pointing to forcible overthrow of government are so identified with conduct that they lose their sheltered position under the First Amendment. According to a majority of the Court, upholding the Smith Act in the *Dennis* case[29] and applying it in the *Yates* case,[30] persons can be punished for participating in conspiratorial activities consisting of speech
· activities that constitute an incitement to present or to future revolutionary acts. The question is whether "the advocacy was aimed at building up a seditious group and maintaining it in readiness for action at a propitious time."[31] Likewise, a person may be punished for individual membership in the Party if again on examination of the record it is demonstrated that his membership is active and purposive by reference to Party activities inciting to future forcible overthrow of government.[32] On the other hand, Justices Black and Douglas hold all advocacy of revolutionary change to be protected by the First

Amendment unless it incites to criminal conduct.[33] Or at the very least they would find speech protected as long as, to use the Holmesian-Brandeis test, it does not present a clear, present, and substantial danger of evils within the power of government to prevent or punish.[34]

In regard to investigations by Congressional committees the difference boils down essentially to the question whether an individual witness can be forced to testify as to Communist membership or association. The majority say "yes" so long as some basis exists for making the question pertinent in the course of the investigation and with respect to this particular witness, since on balance the Congressional interest in disclosure outweighs the individual's right to privacy and the possible harassments and disabilities resulting from disclosure.[35] Here the minority hold that such interrogation and compulsory disclosure subject a person to harassment in the exercise of his First Amendment freedoms and that the real purpose is not to expose Communism but to expose and punish persons for entertaining unpopular views.

Finally, on the matter of forcing disclosure of Communist affiliation as a condition of public employment or as a condition of admission to the bar, the majority—proceeding on a premise that there are appropriate public interests served by excluding from public employment and the legal profession persons who belong to a party that advocates forcible overthrow—hold that it is at least relevant to make the inquiry.[36] On this question the minority hold that to deny a valuable privilege to a person because he refuses to testify respecting Communist affiliation is again to impose disabilities on a person because of his beliefs, absent any grounds for believing that he is engaging in any illegal activities.

Judicial Techniques in Interpretation of the First Amendment
—Absolutism versus the Balancing of Interests

The differences within the Court on these questions reflect a basic difference in judicial philosophy and judicial technique in the exercise of the power of the judicial review. They are the differences between judicial moderation and self-restraint, on the one hand, and judicial activism, on the other. It is the difference between an approach that attempts to strike a balance between the freedom of the First Amendment and the power of government to protect appropriate public interests and an approach that views the First Amendment freedoms as absolute and any abridgment of them as unconstitutional. It is the difference between justices who attempt a judicial neutrality in weighing competing constitutional values and those who identify themselves more fully with the freedom of the individual as against the claims of government. It is the difference between an empiric and pragmatic theory of constitutional interpretation in the reconciliation of freedom and power and a conceptual or definitional theory of interpretation.

The First Amendment says that Congress shall make no law respecting an abridgment of freedom of religion, or of speech, or of the press, or of the right of the people peaceably to assemble and to petition Congress for the redress of grievances. The language of the First Amendment is categorical. On its face it admits of no exception. Any law which abridges any of these freedoms is prohibited. In respect to the interpretation of this language, we may on the whole detect three schools of thinking within the Court. Justices Black and Douglas have taken the position that the First Amendment

means exactly what it says, namely, that Congress shall make
no law respecting an abridgment of these freedoms and that
any law that is recognized to be an abridgment is unconstitutional and that no considerations of public interest can be
considered by the Court in support of legislation that is found
to constitute such an abridgment whether by federal or state
legislation.[37] It is fair to say that Chief Justice Warren has
identified himself with this group and probably Justice
Brennan, too, although they have not expressed their position
as unequivocally as Justices Black and Douglas have done.
But at least it is apparent that their sympathies run in this
direction. Justice Frankfurter, who has not accepted the
thesis at times stated by the Court that the First Amendment
freedoms are preferred or that legislation impinging on these
freedoms is not presumed to be constitutional, applies in interpretation of the First Amendment the same general theory
which Justice Holmes developed in the interpretation of the
Due Process Clause of the Fourteenth Amendment, namely,
that these freedoms are subject to a rational exercise of the
legislative power in the advancement of constitutionally permissible objectives and that so long as it is evident that Congress has acted in a reasonable way, the Court in deference to
the position of the legislature is obliged to uphold the legislation.[38] Associated with the Frankfurter view but not completely identifiable with it is the balance-of-interest theory
which has been advanced principally by Justice Harlan of
the present Court and which in a number of cases has received
support of a majority including that of Justice Frankfurter.[39]
We may, therefore, for all practical purposes reduce the problem to a distinction between the absolute interpretation of
the First Amendment represented by the Black-Douglas school
and the interpretation which permits the Court to balance the

interests and decide where the greater interest lies in a given case. The theory of balance of interests represents a wholly pragmatic approach to the problem of First Amendment freedoms, indeed, to the whole problem of constitutional interpretation. It rests on the theory that it is the Court's function in the case before it when it finds public interests served by legislation on the one hand, and First Amendment freedoms affected by it on the other, to balance the one against the other and to arrive at a judgment where the greater weight shall be placed. If on balance it appears that the public interest served by restrictive legislation is of such a character that it outweighs the abridgment of freedom, then the Court will find the legislation valid. In short, the balance-of-interests theory rests on the basis that constitutional freedoms are not absolute, not even those stated in the First Amendment, and that they may be abridged to some extent to serve appropriate and important public interests. It is by application of this judicial technique that a majority of the Court have sustained the conspiracy and knowing membership sections of the Smith Act, the power of a Congressional committee to require disclosure by a witness of Communist affiliation, and the power of a state to require an applicant for admission to the bar to answer questions respecting Communist affiliation.

Justice Black in recent opinions has not minced words in making an attack on the balance-of-interests technique which as he sees it serves as a judicial device which sanctions intrusions upon and erosion of the First Amendment freedoms.[40] Under the guise of balancing interests, according to Justice Black, the Court has completely undermined the purpose and significance of the First Amendment. In this connection he points to the conclusion reached in recent cases where on balance the Court has almost invariably sustained legislation in the face of assertion of First Amendment rights. According to Justice Black the framers did all the needed balancing when they drafted the First Amendment, and there is no reason for further judicial balancing within the Amendment. On the other hand, Justice Harlan, the spokesman for the balance-of-interests theory, has taken the position that it is true as a matter of general constitutional history and interpretation that no constitutional rights are absolute and that the First Amendment must be construed also by reference to appropriate conceptions of countervailing public interests.

In examination and appraisal of these two schools of thought, it should at first be noted that what is called the absolute interpretation of the First Amendment is not really as absolute as might otherwise appear. The language of the First Amendment is that Congress shall make no law respecting an abridgment of freedom of speech. But conceding that the freedoms coming within a literal reading are absolute, two very important questions remain for interpretation, and in the end it is this interpretation which will be significant. What is included within the category of freedom of speech, and, second, when do we have an abridgment of freedom of speech? The same questions are applicable, of course, with respect to freedom of press and freedom of religion. It is obvious that the reach of the Amendment and the absoluteness of the freedoms are determined by defining the content of these freedoms and, second, defining an abridgment. As noted in the preceding chapter, the Court said in the *Roth* and *Alberts* cases[41] that obscene publication did not come within the free press guarantee, hence, at least in theory it should not raise any question under the First Amendment. Similarly, the Court has said that libelous publications and so-called fighting words do not come within the free press guarantee. In other words, a literal

interpretation of the First Amendment or the so-called absolute interpretation is a definitional or conceptual approach
which seeks to find the meaning of words and to apply this in
a literal way.

It may be questioned, however, whether the absolute or
literal approach does not invoke a balance of interests even
though it is not so manifest on the surface. When the Court
said in the *Roth* and *Alberts* cases that while obscene publication was not protected under freedom of the press, nevertheless, in order to keep this kind of legislation within bounds, a
restrictive definition would be adopted, the Court in effect
was balancing interests by saying that it would take into account a legitimate interest served by obscenity publication
as opposed to the legitimate freedom in this area and that the
point of balance would be determined by the test the Court
enunciated in regard to what is meant by obscene publication.
Similarly, with respect to freedom of religion under the First
Amendment. What is meant by that? The Court has indicated
that it does not include a number of things such as the right
of a person to practice polygamy in the face of a law to the
contrary,[42] the right to employ children to distribute literature
in the face of a child labor law,[43] the right to exemption from
Sunday laws as a matter of freedom of conscience.[44] Why
not? Is it because these are not legitimate exercises of freedom
of religion and that a law restricting them is not an abridgment?
On the absolute interpretation theory it must be either that
these are not included in the free exercise of religion or
that these laws do not constitute an abridgment. Again it may
be suggested that in reaching any results here there is a balance
of interest.

This is emphasized when we turn to the problem of interpreting the second vital term—what is an *abridgment* of

freedom of religion, or of freedom of speech? Does every restriction or every imposition of any disability involve an
abridgment? Obviously, this does not seem to be the case.
At least it must be recognized that the term abridgment is
capable of a broad construction or of narrow construction. It
may refer only to direct abridgment in the sense that it refers
to legislation directed against speech or press or religion as such
and, therefore, does not include indirect abridgments where
Congress or the states are concerned with appropriate public
interests, and application of the legislation does have an indirect effect on the exercise of these freedoms through the
imposition of disabilities that affect them, although not operating as a direct abridgment. Thus, it may be said that to inquire
of a person whether he is a Communist as a condition of his
being admitted to the bar is not an abridgment of freedom of
speech even though it imposes a disability on the person by
reference to speech considerations. The same may be said
of an inquiry by a Congressional committee in respect to a
man's affiliation with the Communist Party. Again, this may
impose disabilities and harass a person in the case of exposure,
but he is still free to speak, to write, and to meet with others
so far as party activity is concerned. In view of the broad questions raised in the interpretation of the First Amendment and
the necessity of fixing and limiting the meanings of the
freedoms there catalogued and the meaning of abridgment,
meanings arrived at by appropriate considerations of public
interest, public policy, history, and tradition, the difference
between the so-called absolutist approach and the avowed
balance-of-interests approach is not as great as one might sus-
pect. There is merit to the Black approach in that it does at
least recognize that within the limits of what is free speech
there can be no abridgment, subject to the interpretation of

what abridgment means. This should not disguise or obscure the fact, however, that a very large measure of subjective judicial evaluation is required in the interpretation of these terms and that neither history, nor words, nor common law gives us a compelling answer and that in the end it is the Court's identification with these values and its conception of its own function in promoting these values that will prove to be the critical elements. In short, it may be suggested that in any interpretation of the First Amendment the judicial appraisal of values and even the emotional response to them—call them prepossessions if you will—play a decisive part whichever theory of construction is used. There are no scientific or objective standards for giving the First Amendment a fixed and determinate meaning.

In defense of the balance-of-interest approach subscribed to by a present majority of the Court, it is accurate to say that it represents the dominant philosophy of constitutional interpretation of the modern era. If there is anything that distinguishes American constitutional interpretation, it is the pragmatic process as distinguished from formal conceptualism or a verbalism that turns on the words used within the four corners of the instrument. This has been the whole history of the Due Process Clause of the Fourteenth Amendment. Indeed, it may be said that the interpretation of the Due Process Clause affords less protection to the substantive liberties than the balance-of-interest technique if due process is interpreted by reference to Justice Holmes' reasonable man. But at least it is clear that over the long run due process has meant an empiric interpretation by the Court based on the facts of the problem before the Court and its weighing of competing interests. This is evident also in other fields of constitutional interpretation and notably in regard to the problems of federal-

ism as they relate to the distribution of powers between the
federal government and the states. The Court has abandoned
all pretense of defining federal powers in conceptual terms
that are designed to place limits on the federal government.
The old idea that commerce meant certain things and that
Congress could not legislate beyond the reach of the powers
so designed has been abandoned by the Court. A determination
by Congress that certain legislation is necessary and proper
in order to carry out certain functions is likely to be sustained
by the Court as long as some rational consideration supports
the Congressional determination, as against the claim that the
subject matter belongs to the reserved powers of the states.[45]
The pragmatic approach by the Court is evidenced particularly
by the cases involving the question of state power to tax and
to regulate commerce. The *Southern Pacific* case[46] gives us an
excellent illustration of the judicial balancing of national and
local interests where the question was raised whether local
legislation interfering with freedom of interstate transportation was valid.

Consider also the interpretation of the provision of the
Fifth Amendment that private property shall not be taken for
public use without just compensation. Although this appears
absolute, still critical questions of construction arise and
within the limits of this language a balancing process takes
place. For instance, the question is raised whether zoning
regulation amounts to a taking of property. The Court has
said this is not a taking,[47] although it is evident that zoning
does in fact impair property interests and does in fact amount
to a taking in the public interest of the uses prohibited to the
owner. The Court has said, however, that this is a reasonable
exercise of the police power, and there is no longer any real
quarrel over the result. What the Court is doing here is

balancing interests in determining what the appropriate public interests are that can be served by police legislation in limiting private property rights and what community interests can be advanced at the expense of private property only by exercise of the condemnation power.[48]

In stating the opinion that the so-called absolute interpretation of the First Amendment is not absolute and that within the range of the literal interpretation there is still wide room for judicial maneuvering which requires an evaluation of competing interests, I do not mean to depreciate an interpretation which seeks to lend pre-eminence to the First Amendment freedoms and which employs the absolute interpretation as a vehicle for achieving this result. On the other hand, I suggest that the balance-of-interest approach is one that finds warrant in the main stream of American constitutional interpretation. If the balance-of-interest technique is to be used, however, it must be done in a way that does justice to constitutional values.

With specific reference to the First Amendment freedoms, the balance-of-interest technique approach affords a useful approach, first of all, in that the Court may more carefully discriminate as to the various facets of freedom there protected. One weakness of the absolute interpretation of the First Amendment and of the general statement that First Amendment freedoms are preferred freedoms is that it tends to ignore the consideration that not all forms of expression stand on the same level in terms of their constitutional importance. Moreover, abridgment may take the form of direct or indirect abridgment, and again this distinction is relevant to the balancing of interests.

It is speech in the sphere of political activities and concerned with matters of public interest that should be the highest and the preferred speech value under the First Amendment. This is the aspect of speech that most clearly distinguishes a democratic society. This includes the freedom to dissent, to express nonconforming ideas, to advocate change, the freedom, indeed, to advocate a new type of social and economic and political structure and to join in political association with others for this purpose. The only justification for laws restricting sedition and advocacy of violent change is that under our system there is abundant opportunity for change by peaceable methods and for this reason the First Amendment freedoms assume a paramount importance in their political aspects. For this reason any approach simply in terms of reasonableness does not do justice to these freedoms as they relate to matters of public concern. The balance-of-interest approach does offer an approach which is consistent with the importance of these freedoms and at the same time is consistent with public interests that may be appropriately served by Congress and the states. The important question is in what way the Court balances these freedoms.

The question may then be raised whether the Court in its decisions dealing with Communists has used the balance-of-interest technique in a way that has undermined and devitalized the First Amendment freedoms. This hardly applies to the recent decision upholding the registration requirement of the Internal Security Act.[49] The public interest in requiring the public identification of a party that is controlled by a foreign government and which has as its objectives the establishment by conspiratorial, revolutionary methods of a Soviet type of dictatorship is clear, and the impact on freedom of political discussion is secondary and indirect. For the same reason there can be no serious objection to the study and examination by a Congressional committee of Communist propaganda and of methods used by the Communist Party in promoting its objectives. Likewise, in view of the nature of the Communist Party, as supported by the determination of the Subversive Activities Control Board, it seems that a substantial public interest warrants an inquiry into Communist affiliation of public employers or of persons seeking admission to the bar.

More difficulty is raised by the decisions upholding the power of a Congressional committee to require a witness to disclose Communist affiliation. In conceding a power of Congress to investigate Communism, it does not necessarily follow that a committee should be allowed to force a man to disclose or deny Communist affiliation at a public hearing which can too easily be converted into a public trial aimed at exposure and without serving any substantial purpose related to the legitimate Congressional interest into the penetration of Communism into various fields of activity. Whether alternative methods are available for achieving the investigative purpose is a factor properly taken into account in any balance of interest. It cannot be seriously argued that Congress or the federal government is without adequate means to inform itself about the Communist movement unless individuals can be forced to disclose their affiliations at a public hearing. The weakness of the *Barenblatt* case[50] in applying the balance-of-interest technique is that the Court did not adequately consider and weigh the necessity of getting the information in this particular way.

The interpretations of the Smith Act relating to the conspiracy and knowing membership clauses present difficulties, too. Admittedly, the governmental interest in protecting against use of violence in the achievement of change is a paramount interest. Too, the fact that concerted activity supports a conspiracy theory is important. But whether the balance should be struck at the point where advocacy is an incitement to future criminal conduct or, as the dissenters contend, at the point where it does in fact incite to criminal conduct, is the problem. Justice Holmes and Brandeis were not absolutists and were ready to balance interests. But in dealing with political speech they balanced speech heavily and required a showing that the speech presented a clear, present, and substantial danger of a public evil within the power of Congress to prohibit or punish. Whether in view of the nature of the Communist conspiracy a lesser test should apply is the question. In this area of speech, where the Court has before it a criminal statute aimed directly at speech, it should be the Court's function in balancing of interests to determine whether, on the record presented to the Court, the danger resulting from the speech is of sufficient weight to warrant the restriction. Certainly, the Court's careful review of the evidence in the *Yates* and *Scales* cases[51] demonstrates that a majority of the Court are not willing to support convictions on the basis alone of participation in Communist Party activities, for some of these activities fall within the sphere of legitimate speech. But even if it is demonstrated that Communists have by their speech incited to future criminal conduct, it should remain open to judicial inquiry whether the danger presented in the case before the Court is of sufficient magnitude to warrant punishment under a criminal statute. It must be remembered that in the cases arising under the Smith Act it is not the Communist Party that is on trial but individual persons charged either with conspiring illegal advocacy or with active and purposive membership in a party guilty of such conspiracy. The question that may well be raised is whether the Court in balancing interests in the Smith Act cases has sufficiently weighed the gravity and substantiality of the danger to the national security on the facts of the case before it in determining where to strike the balance between protected and unprotected speech.

The basic issue involved in this whole area of constitutional adjudication is the question of the wise and proper use of judicial power in reconciling power and freedom. Whatever the formal doctrinal apparatus employed in dealing with the problem, the judge's own basic predisposition and his conception of the judicial power will play influential parts.

There is certainly a respectable line of authority and tradition to support the view that since the power of judicial review is an extraordinary power it should be sparingly exercised, particularly when faced with the question of Congressional authority, and that in the case of such a conflict the Court should be slow to set aside the expression of the legislative will. On the other hand, there is the view that the whole purpose of a written constitution and the institution of judicial review is to enforce restraints against the government and that a court should not be inhibited by the sense of self-restraint or in deference to the legislative determination. And certainly the extent to which the judge identifies himself with certain constitutional values and lifts them to a high point in his thinking will, in turn, govern his decision on specific issues. This dilemma and, in turn, the high degree of judicial subjectivity involved in the whole process of review create the problem which as far as I can see will always persist as long as we have judicial review of legislation. This problem becomes particularly acute when we consider the First Amendment freedoms and the vital place they play in our democratic society. Certainly, the eloquent essays written by Justices Black and Douglas in the wake of earlier opinions by Holmes and Brandeis strike a responsive note in terms of the place of

these freedoms in our open society and demonstrate the utility
also of a theory of freedom that permits the widest exchange
of ideas as the life blood of a democratic society.

It is understandable, however, that a majority of the Court,
mindful of the ultimate responsibility of Congress for determining national policy and enacting appropriate measures for
the national security, should be reluctant to engage in a head-
on collision with Congress on these issues. Over the long run,
as our constitutional history demonstrates, dominant forces
of public opinion will play their part in constitutional interpretation. As has been suggested, the Court best performs its
functions when it nudges and pulls at Congress rather than
coming squarely to battle with it.[52] And it may also be suggested that the greatest function the Court can perform in
these cases, where free speech is an issue, is to employ its
power of statutory interpretation and its review of concrete
cases in a way that will maximize free speech and limit the
operation of restrictive statutes. The importance of this function should not be underestimated, although it is too often
obscured by debate and discussion of ultimate questions of
constitutional power. By a careful and restrictive interpretation of statutes impinging on First Amendment freedoms and
by its own review of the record as well as by the insistence
upon scrupulous observance of procedural regularities, the
Court can make a very effective contribution to the maintenance of these freedoms without precipitating a direct conflict
with Congress. The Court can hold the Smith Act constitutional and still give its provisions a restrictive interpretation.
It can uphold a broad investigative power by Congress and
still find that a committee has not been authorized to act in a
particular way or to inquire into a particular matter. In
case of statutory ambiguity, it can resolve the doubts in favor

of a construction that avoids a constitutional issue. Thus, in the case arising under the knowing membership clause of the Smith Act, the Court might well have found that Congress by a provision in the Internal Security Act had intended to grant immunity to members of the Communist Party from criminal liability based on party membership. Finally, in view of the grounds and theories of statutory interpretation relied upon to sustain the convictions in *Dennis* and *Scales,* the question could well be raised whether the defendants in these cases were properly apprised at the time of indictment and trial of the nature of the offense charged against them.

It is clear that we have adequate vehicles at present for dealing with Communists. Whether the statutes and other measures directed against them represent a wise or necessary use of governmental power is another question. That these measures are constitutional does not answer the question whether they are wise measures. Full exposure of Communism and its techniques and objectives serves a vital and useful purpose. But the usefulness or even desirability of criminal prosecutions under the Smith Act as a means of combating Communism is another matter. No one can doubt the seriousness of the threat that Communism presents to the free and democratic society we cherish. This is a global problem. Mr. Khrushchev predicts the collapse and burial of our type of society. Whether this expectation will be realized will depend not on whether we put a few Communists in jail but on the vitality and strength of our democratic system. Communism thrives on ignorance, poverty, and oppression. Rather than proceed from fear in our tactics and running the risk of driving domestic Communists underground, we do much better to proceed on a positive basis and challenge Communism in the open market place of ideas. In this battle we serve our cause best by shoring up democracy at home, maintaining a system that respects human dignity, is responsive to human needs, honors the basic liberties and a man's freedom to pursue his way, to make his daily choices, and to achieve his potentialities in a free, open, and pluralistic society. Our loyalty and devotion to these values, joined with sensitivity to and compassion for all peoples struggling to escape poverty, disease, ignorance, and exploitation, and an active program of effective assistance in the realization of these objectives, are the weapons for the positive attack in the battle we face. We must give them a sharp cutting edge.

IV. PRIVATE AND GOVERNMENTAL ACTIONS: FLUID CONCEPTS

The current interest in the enforcement of equal rights as protected by the Fourteenth Amendment points up a question that is assuming increasing relevancy and importance. The Fourteenth Amendment reads: ". . . nor shall any State deprive any person of life, liberty or property, without due process of law; nor deny to any person within its jurisdiction the equal protection of the laws." When does a *state* deprive a person of life, liberty, or property without due process of law, or when does a *state* deny a person the equal protection of its laws? The problem is best illustrated by reference to situations and events of wide current interest. If a state court finds Negroes guilty under a state trespass statute because they have staged a sit-in demonstration in a restaurant or at a lunch counter in protest against a policy of not serving Negroes, is the conviction invalid on the ground that the state is guilty of discriminatory action? Or if a state or a local government unit leases publicly owned property or facilities to a private person who practices discriminatory policies, is there a violation of the Fourteenth Amendment? A similar question is raised if real estate dealers licensed under state authority refuse to entertain or to report offers made by Negroes with respect to the purchase of property listed with them. A like problem arises under the Due Process Clause of the Fourteenth Amendment. Obviously, when a private person perpetrates a murder, we do not speak of this as a deprivation of life without due process of law and no question is raised under the Fourteenth Amendment. If, however, a group of persons acting in concert assault a person and cause his death, do we here have something that comes within the range of the Fourteenth Amendment? Or if authorities charged with the duty of maintaining peace and order default in this duty and permit unlawful assaults upon persons and property and interference with their rights to life, liberty, and property, has the state denied these persons due process of law or denied them the equal protection of the laws?

To suggest the questions and illustrations put above is to indicate the importance, currency, and range of the questions. Supreme Court decisions in recent years have dealt with various phases of this problem and contribute to make the subject one of vital, contemporary interest. It may be expected, too, that further phases of this question will reach the Supreme Court in the near future.

In this chapter we shall deal with the question of "state action," indicate the scope of the question, and discuss the question in the context of specific problems as they have arisen before our courts and as they are likely to come before them in the near future.[1]

Fourteenth Amendment as a Restraint on Governmental Actions—General Considerations

At the outset it will be useful again to refer to the express language of the Fourteenth Amendment. Most of the questions we shall deal with are concerned with the Equal Protection Clause, which says that no state shall "deny" to any person the equal protection of the laws. Emphasis on the word "deny" is important. The problem is often stated in terms of "state action," that is, has the state acted in such a way as to offend the Equal Protection Clause? While the term "state action" is useful as a convenient expression for designating the basic problem, it is important to observe that the Constitution does not use the word "action," a word which is really misleading because it suggests that a violation of the Equal Protection Clause can arise only when the state acts in some affirmative way. It is well to emphasize the use of the word "deny," since denial of equal rights may occur either by positive action or by failure of the state to act in an appropriate way in a given situation.

The Equal Protection Clause of the Fourteenth Amendment is paralleled by the more specific provision of the Fifteenth Amendment which says that neither the states nor the United States shall abridge the right to vote because of race, color, or previous condition of servitude. Here, again, the constitutional offense occurs only when the government, either federal or state, abridges the right. Similarly, the Bill of Rights states limitations on the federal government and is not a source of rights directly enforceable against private persons.

In short, the limitations in the interest of the basic freedoms recognized by the Constitution are directed against the government. The Constitution is concerned with constitutional liberties in the classic sense of the Western world, i.e., as liberties of the individual to be safeguarded against the power of the state. It is because the state enjoys the monopoly of lawfully granted coercive power that restraints on its power are recognized under the Constitution as the important conditions of liberty. The Constitution, accordingly, is not concerned with direct restraints on the individual in the interest of defining his duties and the reciprocal rights of his neighbors. Civil rights, as used in the sense that one person has a claim upon another, are the product of common law and legislation—they furnish the staple of the private law of contracts, torts, and property, and of a large and increasing body of public statutory law, including the large mass of criminal law. The substance of my right to contract, to own and enjoy the use of property, to go my way in the pursuit of my daily business free from assaults and interferences by others, and the remedies for the vindication of these rights are defined for me by state law. If X robs me, this is a crime and a tort but not a taking or deprivation of my property in violation of the Constitution, and if I, in turn, deny entrance to my premises to a Jehovah's Witness intent on propagating his faith, I do not violate his constitutionally guaranteed freedom of religion. Civil rights legislation may alter private rights and duties as recognized by the private law. It may impose on employers, or restaurant owners, or landlords a duty not to discriminate on the basis of race, color, religion, or national ancestry, but this result achieved by legislation should not be confused with what the Constitution requires.

It is important at the threshold of this discussion to point out and emphasize that the problem we are primarily concerned with here is the direct impact of the Fourteenth Amendment as interpreted and enforced by the Supreme Court. What we are dealing with is the problem of direct judicial enforcement of the restraint imposed by the Fourteenth Amendment on the states in regard to equal protection and due process of law. It seems clear that under these clauses there is no room for direct judicial intervention unless the claim is made that the state is identified with denial of due process or equal protection. The reference to direct judicial enforcement assumes significance when it is observed that the Fifth Section of the Fourteenth Amendment gives to Congress the power to enforce these limitations by appropriate measures. As an original proposition it would not necessarily follow that the scope of the Fourteenth Amendment restriction as determined by direct judicial interpretation and enforcement determines the scope of the legislative power of Congress to enforce these restrictions. Since the Fifth Section of the Fourteenth Amendment is a grant of power to Congress, it can well be argued that this probably reflected the intent of the drafters of the Amendment that Congress in enforcing the Fourteenth Amendment might resort to legislation it found necessary and proper not only as a means of compelling the observance by the states of their duties in according due process and equal protection of the laws, but also as a means of implementing the underlying policy by creating basic civil rights enforceable against private persons as well. This conclusion is fortified by the well-known historical consideration that one reason for the adoption of the Fourteenth Amendment was to validate and sanction earlier civil rights legislation under which Congress had imposed a duty on persons engaged in certain types of business to treat all persons alike without regard to race and color. If this section of the Fourteenth Amendment had been given the same latitude of interpretation that other Congressional legislative powers enjoy, according to the rule of liberal interpretation as stated by Chief Justice Marshall in *McCulloch* v. *Maryland*,[2] it is readily conceivable that Congress would have the authority to enact civil rights legislation directed not only against the states but also against private persons, on the theory that legislation imposing a duty on private persons to respect certain basic rights would implement the general policy of the Fourteenth Amendment, which in its central aspect was designed to establish the constitutional status of Negroes and secure their equal rights.

When the question first came before the Supreme Court in the famous *Civil Rights Cases*,[3] decided by the Court during the period of *rapprochement* between North and South, the Court, with only Justice Harlan dissenting, interpreted the Fifth Section of the Fourteenth Amendment to be a source to Congress only of a corrective power to deal with violations by the states of the restrictions imposed on them by the Equal Protection and Due Process clauses. The Court found that while Congress could under the Fifth Section enact appropriate remedial legislation by way of penalties and civil remedies directed against those who acting under authority of law were responsible for denying a person the equal protection of the laws or depriving him of his life, liberty, and property without due process, it could not reach private conduct and create private rights. This decision, of course, severely and closely limited the power of Congress to enact civil rights legislation at least insofar as its authority is grounded on the Fourteenth Amendment. In his dissenting opinion, Mr. Justice Harlan protested vehemently against a construction of the Congressional power which he thought curtailed and restricted the power in a way that was not intended.

As a result of the *Civil Rights Cases*, both the courts and Congress in enforcing the Equal Protection and Due Process clauses of the Fourteenth Amendment are limited to dealing with cases where it is charged that the state through use of its lawfully constituted agencies or officers has denied a person equal protection or due process of law. The practical effect of this has been that the judiciary has assumed the dominant role both in defining the meaning of the Equal Protection and Due Process clauses and in enforcing sanctions designed to compel observance by the states of the rights protected by these clauses. Congress has discharged its role by giving the Supreme Court appellate jurisdiction in cases originating in the state courts where federal questions are raised, by giving the lower federal courts jurisdiction to deal with federal-question cases, and by enacting special remedial and criminal statutes furnishing a basis for civil and criminal proceedings in federal courts when a person claims a deprivation or denial of constitutional rights by persons acting under "color of law." The Congressional role in these matters will be developed more fully in the final chapter. It is the judiciary, however, that occupies the key role in the enforcement of the Equal Protection and Due Process clauses, and it has exercised this role chiefly by direct enforcement through the judicial process. And even if the Court were to depart from the *Civil Rights Cases* in the future and accord to Congress an enforcement power that included a power to enact substantive civil rights legislation, it is still clear that there can be no direct judicial enforcement of the Fourteenth Amendment without a finding that a state has been party to a denial of due process or equal protection.

In order to avoid leaving an erroneous impression at this point and at the risk of duplicating in part what will be developed at greater length in the concluding chapter, it should be made clear that Congress in acting to create or protect individual rights is not limited to the power it possesses to enforce the Equal Protection and Due Process clauses. The various substantive legislative powers of Congress, such as the power to regulate commerce, to regulate the status of aliens, to spend money for the general welfare, and to enact legislation for the territories, may be employed as a means of creating basic rights and assuring their protection against both public and private impairment. Likewise, Congress can enact appropriate legislation to provide civil and criminal sanctions against private persons interfering with the right to vote for federal officers or otherwise interfering with the enjoyment of the privileges and immunities of natural citizenship. What we are discussing at this point is the interpretation and enforcement of the Fourteenth Amendment as a command to the states to accord equal protection and due process to persons within their jurisdiction. The task of giving meaning and vitality to this command has been assumed by the Supreme Court.

In its review of state court decisions or of lower federal court decisions that raise the equal protection and due process issues, the Supreme Court must find the element of "state action" in the case, whether it be affirmative action or the failure to act. It continues to be true now, as it was when the *Civil Rights Cases* were decided, that private action raises no equal protection or due process question unless it is sanctioned by the state in a way that involves one of the organs or processes of state power.

The Equal Protection and Due Process clauses operate as a restraint on all branches of the state government—legislative, executive, and judicial—and on all officers and agencies purporting to act under state authority. In a very elementary sense, therefore, it may be said that the jurisdictional requirement of state action is satisfied as soon as it is shown that a person's rights or liberties are affected by a law or an act or omission to act on the part of anyone acting by authority of the state. If a person is arrested by a police officer and tried and convicted by a state judge on a criminal charge brought under criminal statute, adequate elements of state action are found in the actions of the policeman and of the court and in the statute enacted by the legislature. Or if a judge enters a decree enjoining violation of a restrictive covenant, the judge's decree is clearly action by the state. But if in the criminal trespass case the owner of the property who filed the complaint is following a policy of discriminating against Negroes at the restaurant operated by the owner, and if the restrictive covenant in the second case is directed against occupancy of property by Negroes, does it follow that the state's involvement in these cases means that the state is guilty of denying the equal protection of its laws? The question, then, when some kind of involvement by a state agency is presented, is not whether there is state action at all. By hypothesis the question must be answered in the affirmative. The real question, then, is whether the state in sanctioning this private conduct is denying equal protection. In short, when the power of government is used in any way to sustain private right, by hypothesis the state is involved and must assume responsibility for the choice made in the resolution of conflicting interests.

The question then remains, however, whether the state action results in a violation of the substantive limitation. This will become apparent from the later discussion. One illustration at this point suffices to point up the problem. If a Jehovah's Witness is convicted under a trespass statute on a charge of repeatedly entering the premises of a person who had made clear his policy of refusing admittance to Jehovah's Witnesses, and if this conviction under state law is held consistent with the Fourteenth Amendment, is the result justified on the ground that the state is not involved in the discrimination against a particular religious sect, or is it justified on the ground that the state in balancing competing rights may here protect the property owner by sanctioning discrimination to this extent against Jehovah's Witnesses? The distinction between whether the state is involved and whether, if it is involved, the choice of values it supports violates constitutional policy, must be kept in mind in any examination and analysis of the case materials.

The Kinds of Governmental Action Limited by the Equal Protection and Due Process Clauses—Legislative Enactments, Executive Acts, and Judicial Determination of Controversies Involving Property and Contract Rights

No substantial problem is raised in respect to identification of legislative action as state action. If a legislature passes a statute requiring segregation of the races in all swimming pools and recreational areas, and a Negro who swims in a pool set aside for whites is arrested and convicted for violating the statute, the state involvement and responsibility are clear since the legislature has initiated and determined the discriminatory policy.

One aspect of the legislative power problem should, however, be noted at this point. The question of what a state legislature is prohibited from doing under the Fourteenth Amendment in the exercise of its law-making power should not be confused or identified with the question of what a state may appropriately do in exercise of its police power to protect rights against private aggression. The fact that a state by its civil and criminal law protects private property and the lives and persons of its citizens is something we have taken for granted. Yet it should be noted that the ordinary private law as well as the criminal law may be viewed as exercises of the state legislative power resulting in the creation of reciprocal private rights and obligations. The state may enact new legislation resulting in a broadened conception of private right.

Thus, a state may at the present time enact antidiscrimination legislation, where the purpose is to prohibit, as well as provide remedies against, discrimination practiced by private persons on the basis of race, color, or religion. That the police power is now viewed as broad enough to encompass these purposes hardly admits of doubt. Thus, there is no difficulty about a state's enacting fair employment legislation or civil rights legislation which prohibits persons engaged in certain types of business, usually open to the public, from discriminating on the basis of race, color, or religion. The point here stressed, however, is that the power of the state to do so is a discretionary power and is not to be confused with a *duty* imposed by the Fourteenth Amendment to enact this kind of legislation. This Amendment imposes no obligation on the states to enact new legislation for the further creation and protection of civil rights, although, as will be pointed out later, state courts in defining public policy considerations relevant to private law cannot ignore the restrictions embodied in this Amendment.

As in the case of legislative acts, so executive and administrative acts of state officers present clear instances of state action when they initiate or administer discriminatory policies. If the governor of a state closes a school because it is ready to pursue a program of desegregation, state action is patently clear. Nor is there any difficulty in characterizing a discriminatory policy pursued by a state administrative agency as unconstitutional state action even if the statute creating and defining the agency's authority does not require or authorize discrimination. For instance, if an officer charged with the dispensation of a privilege under a statute, such as the licensing of a given business, follows a practice of discriminating on the basis of race in the dispensation of licenses, proof of this practice is sufficient to demonstrate an unlawful discrimination by the state. The Court said in the famous case of *Yick Wo* v. *Hopkins*[4] that the law may be administered with an evil eye and an uneven hand. This principle has received its greatest application in recent years in the cases dealing with the problems of discrimination against Negroes with respect to jury service. In a number of instances the Supreme Court has found unlawful discrimination against Negroes where the evidence clearly demonstrated that, despite the availability of Negroes for jury service, no Negro had been called for service in a given county or unit over a long period of time.[5]

The active participation by the state in the administration of property owned or held in trust by it raises the same question. In the *Girard Trust* case[6] the Supreme Court held invalid a municipality's participation as trustee in the administration of a trust set up to establish a school for the benefit of poor white orphans. The state and its political subdivisions cannot be actively engaged in the administration of a program that denies equal protection. The significance of the state's role in administering the Girard Trust was highlighted by the subsequent action taken by the City of Philadelphia in relieving itself of the trusteeship and having a private trust appointed in order to carry out the terms of the trust. The Supreme Court, thereafter, refused to review the state court's approval of this change.[7] Apparently neither the administration of this trust by private persons nor the state's action in facilitating private administration was seen to raise substantial constitutional questions.

A further aspect of administrative or executive discrimination may be found in the failure on the part of those charged with legal duties to carry them out where this failure is attributable to discriminatory motives. It is at this point that it becomes important to remember that the Fourteenth Amendment makes it unlawful for a state to deny to persons the equal protection of its laws, and that official failure to carry out a duty, call it "state inaction," if you will, may come within the condemnation of the Fourteenth Amendment as well as positive action. No one doubts that if a state judge refuses to entertain a cause of action because it is brought by a Negro, this would be a blatant case of denial of equal protection by the state. It should be equally clear that if a police officer, who is charged with the duty of protecting property and preventing breach of the public peace, deliberately fails to use his authority to protect the persons or property of Negroes against violence or assault, the state through its lawfully constituted agency is here denying equal protection of the laws. Negroes are not being given the same equal security under the law as whites are. Where a clear case is presented of deliberate failure of state peace officers to protect the person or property of certain persons or groups of persons, it should be appropriate for a federal court to issue a mandatory injunction compelling the performance of constitutional duty.

The recognition that the requisite state action is found in the actions of the state administrative and executive officers exercising state authority raises the interesting and more difficult question whether the state is to be identified with the lawless action of its officers. If, for instance, a sheriff or a police officer is guilty of undue violence in his treatment of a prisoner, causing either injury or death to the prisoner, does this amount to unconstitutional conduct on the theory that a state agent has acted to deprive a person of his life without due process of law or is this a case of private murder punishable only under state law? It may appear anomalous to suggest that when a person acting under authority of state law abuses his position and acts not only without authority but in contravention of state law and thereby commits a criminal act, his action, nevertheless, is to be identified with the state. Yet, the Supreme Court of the United States in the well-known *Screws* case[8] held that a sheriff who had abused a prisoner and caused his death was liable under the federal criminal statute directed against persons who acting under color of law subject the inhabitant of a state to the deprivation of any rights, privileges, or immunity secured or protected by the Constitution or laws of the United States. Over the protest of dissenting judges who declared that lawless action cannot be identified with action under color of law and that the effect of the Court's holding would be to weaken a state's own responsibility for dealing with lawless individuals, the majority of the Court, speaking through Mr. Justice Douglas, held that the fact that the arrest was made by a person clothed with the authority of law sufficiently identified his action with the state's authority and thereby raised his lawless conduct to the level of unconstitutional action. It is quite clear that this is one of the cases that must be included in a list of cases of recent vintage that have marked a steady progression in the expansion of the state action concept, with the result of giving the Fourteenth Amendment a broader reach. It is true that the *Screws* case arose under a federal statute, but in view of the Court's adherence to the basic holding of the *Civil Rights Cases*, it must be assumed that the color of law concept employed in this statute is identified by the Court with the state action concept derived from the Fourteenth Amendment.

The theory of the *Screws* case was affirmed recently by the Court in *Monroe* v. *Pape*,[9] where it held that city police officers guilty of an unreasonable search and seizure, in violation of the due process guarantee, were liable in a civil action for damages brought by the injured person under authority of a federal statute giving a cause of action against any person who under color of law deprives a person of his constitutional rights. The larger part of the Court's opinion was devoted to the question of statutory interpretation. There was no doubt in the majority opinion about the constitutional power of Congress to reach this kind of conduct pursuant to the Congressional power to enforce the Fourteenth Amendment.

"There can be no doubt at least since *Ex parte Virginia*, that Congress has the power to enforce provisions of the Fourteenth Amendment against those who carry a badge of authority of a State and represent it in some capacity, whether they act in accordance with their authority or misuse it."[10]

Justices Harlan and Stewart, concurring separately, felt that the case was controlled by the *Classic*[11] and *Screws*[12] cases, although they expressed doubt whether these earlier cases were correctly decided in the first instance on the question of statutory interpretation. Justice Frankfurter, dissenting at length on the question of statutory interpretation, repeated in substance the views he had previously stated in dissent in the *Screws* case.

We come now to the judicial branch of the state government and the relevancy of its authority and action with respect to the restraints imposed by the Fourteenth Amendment. We start with the propositions that every judicial officer is a state officer and that a state court's action is state action in the most elementary sense. Thus, if a judicial officer has the authority to select jurors and is clearly guilty of discriminations in the exercise of this ministerial power, his action, whether or not pursuant to statutory authority, is as invalid under the Equal Protection Clause as that of an administrative or executive officer.[13] Likewise, if a state judge, conducting the trial of a criminal case, conducts the trial in such a way that it lacks the elements of a fair trial, it is clear that the state through the judge has deprived the prisoner of his right to due process of law. Likewise, as suggested above, if a state court, in granting or denying a cause of action, discriminates on the basis of race, the state is guilty of a denial of equal protection.

More subtle and difficult questions are raised, however, when we turn to the function of a state court in defining and interpreting the rights and duties of private persons in areas governed by the law of property or contracts. The judiciary in discharging its creative and interpretative role with respect to the substance of the law may be functioning jointly with the other organs of state power. If, for instance, a Negro engaged in a sit-in demonstration is arrested on a charge of violating a general and nondiscriminatory criminal trespass statute and is convicted on this charge by a state court, all three organs of state power—the legislative, the executive, and the judicial—may be said to be involved and certainly there is no lack of state action in the elementary sense. Whether the use of the state's coercive power to support private discrimination violates the Equal Protection Clause becomes the critical question. In the end, the state court's interpretation of the statute as well as its interpretation of the rights of property owners will be the most conspicuous aspects of the state action present in this picture. It is the role of the courts, however, in fashioning the state's common law and thereby defining private rights and obligations, rather than the judicial role in statutory interpretation, which most clearly and dramatically goes to the heart of the problem whether judicial enforcement of private rights which has the effect of sanctioning discriminatory policies initiated and pursued by private persons is prohibited by the Equal Protection

Clause. Again, it should be emphasized that the question in case of a court judgment or decree, founded on the recognition of private contractual or proprietary rights, is not whether there is state action, but whether it is state action identified with denial of equal protection.

In two types of situations involving claims of denial of constitutional right because of application of judicially developed substantive law, the identification of the judiciary with the denial of constitutional right is beyond dispute. The first category presents the case where a court relieves a person pursuing a discriminatory policy from the operation of a judge-made general rule. The common law doctrine, still in force in some states, that common carriers and innkeepers are under a duty to serve all without discrimination furnishes a prime illustration. Under this general rule a person who applies to an innkeeper (nowadays a hotel) for accommodations and is refused has a cause of action for damages suffered as the result of the innkeeper's breach of his common law duty. Suppose, then, that service is refused a person solely because he is a Negro in accordance with the innkeeper's policy of serving whites only. A damage action is then brought in a state court by the Negro. If the state court now holds that consistent with a general duty to serve all comers, the innkeeper may adopt reasonable rules and regulations; that it is reasonable to exclude Negroes as a class, is this a case of state denial of equal protection? This seems clearly to be the case. In effect the court is saying that even though the law recognizes a general duty to serve all, it still will not give a cause of action to a Negro who has been discriminated against. Or to put the matter another way, the law gives to whites a right to service which is denied to Negroes. Nor is it an adequate answer to say that the law permits reasonable classification, since a classification that results in discrimination against Negroes is not permissible. The important point to be stressed in this situation is that, apart from a limiting classification established by the carrier and sanctioned by the court, there is an independent right created by law to be served. To deny this right by reference to race or color is to permit a state sanctioned discrimination, the same as if a statute had been imposed on innkeepers to serve all but with the provision that an innkeeper could at his discretion refuse to serve members of a particular class determined by race or color.

The Court's recent decision in *Burton v. Wilmington Parking Authority*[14] deserves attention at this point. This case dealt with the question whether a person operating a restaurant in an off-street parking structure pursuant to a lease from a public parking authority was under a constitutional duty to serve Negroes. The Court upheld the duty. A majority rested the result on the ground that in view of the circumstances attending the lease of this public property the state's participation and involvement in the policy of discriminating against Negroes was such that this presented a case of state denial of equal protection. In this aspect the case will receive further attention later. Of special interest here is Justice Stewart's brief separate opinion in which he supported the result on the wholly different ground that a Delaware statute which had been brought into the case had been interpreted by the Delaware Supreme Court as authorizing restaurants to establish a discriminatory classification based exclusively on color. Justice Stewart's position rests on the assumption that the Delaware statute did create a general duty on the part of restaurant owners to serve the public. Justices Harlan and Whittaker agreed that if Justice Stewart's interpretation of the state court's action in construing the statute was correct, the state was guilty of denying equal protection, but they were not sure that the Delaware statute modified the common law rule that a restaurant owner could serve whom he pleased. Accordingly, they were in favor of sending the case back for clarification of the state law question.

Although only three justices dealt with this phase of the problem, it can hardly be supposed that the majority would have disagreed on the proposition that a statute which imposes a duty to serve all but authorizes discrimination based on race violates the Equal Protection Clause. Nor would it make any difference if the general duty to serve and the corresponding limitation by race or color are established by judge-made, as distinguished from statutory, law.

In the type of case just discussed a court sanctions private discrimination at the expense of an independent right created by law. Basically the same pattern is recognizable in a second type of situation. A state court in order to protect a movie operator's proprietary interest issues an injunction against peaceful picketing by persons who are protesting the showing of the movie. Whatever may be the decision on the merits of the case, it is clear here that the state through the judiciary is restraining freedom of speech, a fundamental right protected under the Due Process Clause. It is no answer to say that the court is acting merely to protect private property rights. When the court in order to protect these rights uses its power to restrict a wholly independent right protected by the Constitution, the state's sanctioning of a restriction on a constitutional freedom is clearly established.[15]

In both cases discussed above, the question does not really turn at all on whether there was state action, but on the issue whether the state is using its power in declaring and enforcing one man's right to interfere with another's freedom. In these

situations the problem rapidly boils down then to a consideration of the competing substantive rights at stake. When the
state—whether through its legislative, executive, or judicial
organs—takes a side in a dispute between private parties, it
cannot avoid responsibility under the Fourteenth Amendment
for the result reached. The consideration alone that a court is
acting to protect contractual or property rights as recognized
by common law or statute is not determinative of the issue,
for the state itself determines the limits of these rights. Contractual and property rights are limited by law. Some contracts
or contractual provisions are unenforceable because they are
opposed to public policy, and the power to use and dispose of
property is not an unlimited one even as a matter of private
property law. A condition attached to a gift or other disposition
of property may be held invalid because it contravenes public
policy. The point is that courts have always taken policy considerations into account in defining the content and scope of
private rights. It follows, therefore, that courts must also take
constitutional policies into account in striking a balance between competing private rights. For a state court to say that
public policy forbids giving a certain reach to private property
or contract rights may be one way of saying that due regard for
constitutional policy requires this result.

Against the background of the ideas just examined, we now
turn to the famous case of *Shelley* v. *Kraemer*,[16] the central
case in any discussion of the constitutional significance of
judicial protection of private interests. In the *Shelley* case the
Court held that judicial enforcement of a racially restrictive
covenant violated the Equal Protection Clause. In this case,
white neighbors sought to enjoin a Negro who had purchased
the property from a previous white owner from occupying the
premises in violation of a deed covenant which restricted occu-

pancy to whites. The state court had not only enjoined the occupancy but had also ordered a rescission of the sale. The Supreme Court in finding the state court's decision a denial of equal protection stated that the state court's action in recognizing and enforcing the covenant bore "the clear and unmistakable imprimatur of the State."[17] The restrictive convenant itself was not unconstitutional and voluntary adherence to it raised no constitutional issue, but the state court could not constitutionally be a party to its enforcement. Moreover, it was no answer that the court was simply protecting property rights according to a general rule and that the state itself was not discriminating since it would in the proper case enforce covenants directed against occupancy by whites. Inequality could not be cured by further compounding inequality.

The *Shelley* case raises in a critical way the question how far a state may go with its judicial machinery in protecting property and contract rights without running afoul the Equal Protection Clause. Certainly there are some factors in the case that serve as distinguishing and limiting elements. First, the point can be made that the Negro, because of his contract, had an independent right, and that but for the court's enforcement of the restrictive covenant he would have had the right to enjoy the use of the property. So viewed, the case means that a court may not at the instance of one party having an interest in property give effect to a privately initiated policy of racial discrimination as a basis for interfering with the independent right of a third person to purchase and use the property—a right recognized as fundamental under the Due Process Clause. It may be questioned if this is an accurate analysis, since any person buying property takes it with notice of and subject to restrictive covenants, so it is questionable whether in case of purchase of this property he has a right to

its use independent of the covenant. In any event, if the inde-
pendent-right interpretation is correct, this serves to distinguish
Shelley from the case where an owner refuses to sell or lease
to a person because of his race or color. In the latter case no
right of any kind can be asserted in respect to the particular
property involved. A second factor in the *Shelley* case is that
the court was giving effect to a collective discrimination as
represented by the restrictive covenant, much the same as if
it were enforcing a city ordinance. To put the matter
another way, the state court was using its power to enforce
a contract which imposed on the parties thereto a duty to
discriminate. Again, this was not the case of one man discriminating as a matter of his own choice in the use of his
own property or business. In the third place, the suit was
initiated by the adjoining property owners, and the state court
in issuing an injunction was using the covenant as a sword
to prevent a person because he was a Negro from enjoying
the use of property which he had purchased and to the use
of which he was entitled but for the covenant. Finally, it may
be suggested that the Court's decision implicitly weighed the
values of the competing interests at stake. The neighboring
property owners were not asserting a right to control the
use and control of their own properties, but the Negro, on
the other hand, was asserting a basic right to own and enjoy
the use of property for the benefit of himself and his family.
Here the state court made an unwarranted choice between
competing values.

Are all these factors important in assessing the significance
of the *Shelley* case, and does the lack of one or more of them
serve to distinguish other cases? Consideration may be given
at this point to the case of *Rice* v. *Sioux City Memorial Park
Cemetery*. Here the defendant cemetery association refused to

permit the interment of an American Indian on the ground that under the express terms of the deed to the lot only Caucasians could be buried. The Supreme Court of Iowa upheld the association's defense in an action for damages brought by the wife of the deceased and distinguished *Shelley* on the ground that there the restrictive covenant was used as a sword whereas here it was used as a shield.[18] By a four-to-four decision and without opinion, the Supreme Court of the United States affirmed the decision.[19] At least four justices, it may be presumed, thought *Shelley* was distinguishable. Should the fact alone that here the deed restriction was asserted as a defense be a sufficient basis for distinguishing *Shelley?* This distinction has some merit even though it appears to place stress on form and type of remedy in the case where private discrimination is sustained by judicial action, but other factors may be noted too. The plaintiff in the cemetery case, in order to sustain her claim, was asking the court to disregard a part of the contract on which her claim was based. Here, there was no independent right on which the plaintiff could rely. Any burial right was derived from and dependent upon the contract and deed which contained the restrictive clause. Moreover, the defendant was not resting its case on a duty to discriminate pursuant to a contract with other persons but instead asserting its privilege to determine the use made of its land. While all of these may be cited as distinguishing factors, it is clear also that four members of the Court, nevertheless, must have thought that *Shelley* controlled and that the problem in the choice of constitutionally recognized values was no different from that of Shelley.

Finally, consider the case of *Black* v. *Cutter Laboratories,*[20] where a majority of the Court found that no federal constitutional issue was raised by a decision of the California Supreme Court holding that membership in the Communist party was "just cause," within the meaning of a collective bargaining agreement, for dismissing an employee. The majority of the Court stated that the case turned on a state court's interpretation of the terms of a contract and therefore rested on an independent ground of state law. A minority of the Court, applying the *Shelley* rationale, found that the state court by its function in interpreting the contract was sanctioning a discrimination against an employee because of his political affiliation and that this violated the Fourteenth and First amendments. Whatever else may be said about this case, it is fair to say that the majority opinion avoided the critical question in which we are interested by saying that the case rested on an independent ground of state law. If the case raises no constitutional issues, it must be for better reasons than those stated by the Court. Certainly the state court's action in interpreting the contract was state action. The question here was whether there was state action that impaired the right of political association. It does not help much to say that the case rested on an independent ground of state law. The same might have been said in *Shelley* v. *Kraemer,* but there the Supreme Court found that the state court's action in enforcing a private contract made the state a party to denial of equal protection. Is *Black,* like *Rice,* distinguishable from *Shelley* on the grounds either that the employer was using the contract as a defense to a dismissal already consummated, or that the defendant's act was voluntary and not a duty imposed on it by a contract with third persons, or that the plaintiff's rights depended entirely on the contract pursuant to which the dismissal was made? Or does the *Black* case suggest that on the meritorious constitutional issue a distinction may be observed between a state court's sanctioning a discrimination against

Negroes with respect to the ownership and enjoyment of property and sanctioning a discrimination against Communists in private employment?

What conclusions then can be drawn from these cases in regard to the judicial enforcement of private rights? Any attempt at generalization is hazardous since it is evident that the Supreme Court itself is still groping its way in this area and has not yet attempted a definitive rationale. But some conclusions may be attempted. First of all, it seems clear that the Court continues to adhere to the distinction between private action in asserting contractual and property rights and judicial action in enforcing these rights. A restrictive covenant directed against occupancy of property by Negroes is not illegal under the Constitution, and property owners if they choose may voluntarily adhere to it, but it is constitutionally unenforceable. This gives us a sharp distinction between right and remedy. The question may well be asked whether it is not the assurance of judicial protection that gives content and meaning to all private right. On this theory every private assertion of right is implicitly vested with the sanction of state authority, but to carry this idea to its logical conclusion would destroy completely the distinction between governmental and private action.

It is clear, however, that since judicial action is state action, all judicial enforcement of private contractual and property rights is potentially subject to attack under the Equal Protection and Due Process clauses of the Fourteenth Amendment and that the really critical question is whether a court in protecting one man's interests is thereby subjecting another person to an unconstitutional impairment of his rights or liberties. Any party complaining that judicial enforcement of private right is unconstitutional must establish that this enforcement impairs his enjoyment of a tangible and concrete right, interest, or liberty recognized at law, whether on the basis of contract, common law, statute, or Constitution. Secondly, even if there is some impairment or damage, it must be shown that this impairment results from an improper choice by the state judiciary in the recognition and interpretation of private rights. The ultimate decision then turns really on a weighing of the merits of the problem. It seems to me that in the end it should not be the form of remedy, the way in which the question arises before courts, or even whether an independent right exists that should control but rather the meritorious quality of the judicial action in choosing between competing interests and freedoms. The owner of property has constitutional rights, too. Just as a legislative enactment defining rights and duties as between private persons is subject to review to determine whether it establishes an unreasonable ·classification or unreasonably interferes with a fundamental right, so a judicial decision interpreting, defining, and enforcing property or contractual rights is subject to review for the purpose of determining whether the court has acted with due and reasonable regard for constitutionally recognized values in striking the balance. To sanction by judicial enforcement a contract whereby persons agree to discriminate against members of a race and thereby even support a duty to discriminate is to weight contract and private right too heavily and makes the court's action unreasonable. To say, however, that a person is free to practice discrimination as a wholly voluntary and private matter is altogether different. Here the balance may be struck in favor of private right. In short, consistent with *Shelley,* private property owners may still be accorded substantial freedom, as vindicated by judicial decision, to determine the use of their property and the terms on which they may contract with others.

In concluding this part where we are distinctively dealing with persons and agencies exercising the authority of the state, we may look at the question of great current interest, namely, whether enforcement of a trespass statute against Negroes who are staging a sit-in demonstration at a lunch counter raises problems of denial of equal protection under the Fourteenth Amendment. It is clear, of course, that a trespass statute on its face is not discriminatory, just as any general criminal law is not discriminatory, and that its enforcement evenhandedly raises no problems.

On the other hand, a trespass statute cannot be enforced at the expense of constitutional rights. Obviously a statute making it a crime for Negroes to enter or remain in certain business establishments would be a patent denial of equal protection. Similarly, if a statute gives a right to persons to enter certain types of privately owned establishments open generally to the public but qualifies the right by permitting the owner to exclude persons whom he regards as offensive, and the owner establishes the rule that no Negroes will be served, enforcement of a trespass action against a Negro should be held unconstitutional, since the statute as interpreted permits the conditioning of a statutory right by reference to a racial classification.[21] And if, in the absence of a statute, the common law of the state recognizes that a person operating an establishment like a restaurant is under a duty to serve the public and yet the state court permits the owner to establish an exception on a racial basis, an equally strong case can be made that the state is making itself a party to racial discrimination with respect to the enjoyment of common right.

But unless by statute or common law a person can claim

a right to enter the premises and be served, it becomes much more difficult to find that the enforcement of a trespass statute results in the denial of constitutional right where the owner discriminates on a racial basis. The Supreme Court may say as a matter of its own characterization that a restaurant which in fact is open to the public generally assumes the aspects of a business affected with a public interest and is therefore under a duty to serve all without discrimination, but it is not likely that the Court will reach an independent determination on what should be a question of state law. This leaves for consideration then the possibility that the Court would find that the action of the state court in finding that a restaurant owner's right to control the use of his property and the choice of his patrons, including the right to exclude on a racial basis, is invalid because the court is improperly protecting private property rights at the expense of one class of citizens. To put the matter this way is to say in different words that the state court is required by the Equal Protection Clause to fashion a rule to the effect that restaurant owners must serve Negroes. It is doubtful that the Supreme Court will or should go this far. Even if we grant that the Court may appropriately inquire whether a state court is acting reasonably in defining property rights and that this inquiry extends to the point of asking whether the state court has struck a proper balance between opposing interests, it remains to determine where the balance should be struck in this case. The owner asserts a right to control his business and to choose his patrons on a basis that will best protect his business. The Negroes are asserting a right to be treated equally with others and to be served on the same basis. Both parties are declaring substantial and important interests. Under these circumstances, since a choice has to be made and since a choice of either interest has some justification, the action of the state in preferring to place its emphasis upon the owner's freedom to choose his patrons can be upheld as a rational exercise of discretionary power in the resolution of conflicting interests. This conclusion, it should be emphasized, is warranted only if it is clear that under local law there is no duty on the part of the owner to serve the public generally, that the result turns wholly on the voluntary action and choice of the owner, and that there are no countervailing circumstances present in the situation, such as monopolistic control, which unduly advantage the owner in carrying on his business and making his choice of customers.

Application of the Fourteenth Amendment Limitations to Private Persons, Groups, or Associations

Up to this point we have been looking at the question of state action by reference to the actions taken by agencies or organs of the government. We now consider a second category of situations where we have actions taken by persons or associations or organizations that may be regarded as private in character but whose relationship to the state by reference to special privileges enjoyed, property used, or position in the state's regulatory scheme may raise questions as to whether their actions are to be identified with the state for purpose of the Fourteenth Amendment restrictions. If their action is to be characterized as state action for purpose of these constitutional restrictions, it must be on an instrumentality or agency theory, i.e., that in one way or another they are to be regarded as exercising power delegated by the state or serving as agents in carrying out state purposes or otherwise so completely identified with state objectives that the state must assume responsibility for their actions. This category embraces several types of enterprise which serve public purposes but are not publicly owned or operated.

A clear case is found in the instance of a private person or company which enjoys a special grant of franchise from the state, whether it be a grant of eminent domain power or an exclusive operating franchise. Public utilities and railroads fall into this category. Railroads enjoy the eminent domain power and so do the recognized public utilities such as electric, gas, telephone, and water companies. The only justification for giving the utilities eminent domain power is that they are in effect discharging a proper function of the state itself, and to view them as agencies of the states for purpose of the Fourteenth Amendment is no stretch or distortion of theory. Moreover, under the characteristically modern scheme of regulation, utilities including motor carriers enjoy a special quasi-monopolistic privilege since each is required to secure a certificate of public convenience and necessity from the governing authorities. It is because of the nature of this business and the enjoyment of special privileges that public utilities and carriers are under duty to serve all of the public alike, so that, even apart from any constitutional duty not to discriminate, these companies are by law subject to a public duty to serve without unjust discrimination. To be sure, the fact that the statute imposes an obligation to serve usually makes it unnecessary to consider the question whether they are guilty of any unconstitutional discrimination. Attention is called at this point to the recent *Boynton* case,[22] where the Supreme Court held that the conviction of a Negro under Virginia's criminal statute for demanding service at a restaurant open to whites only was invalid, since under the Interstate Commerce Act[23] the Negro, a passenger on an interstate bus, had the right to be served at the restaurant which the Court had found was a part of the interstate transportation facilities.

It is true that in the early *Civil Rights Cases*[24] the Court found invalid the federal statute which imposed a duty on common carriers as well as innkeepers and theater owners to serve all without discrimination based on race or color. However, attention was not given by the Court to the consideration that common carriers insofar as they were railroads did enjoy special facilities and franchises that serve as a basis for identifying their action with that of the state. Mr. Justice Harlan in his dissenting opinion did refer to this, and it hardly seems doubtful at the present time that the instrumentality theory would be validly applied in this situation. In this connection a question may be raised respecting a fairly recent decision by the New York Court of Appeals. Here, the state had granted the eminent domain privilege, certain tax advantages, and the privilege of vacating certain public streets to a private corporation authorized to develop a large-scale housing project. The United States Supreme Court chose not to review the decision by the New York Court of Appeals that the company was not subject to the constitutional rule against discrimination.[25] It is surprising, indeed, that a company enjoying these grants of special privilege, including the eminent domain power, should be free to determine its practices as though it were a strictly private corporation.

A question arising frequently these days is whether the private lessee of property owned by a state or one of its subdivisions is bound by the restrictions of the Fourteenth Amendment. In some cases it may appear that the leasing of the property was done deliberately for the purpose of avoiding a Fourteenth Amendment restriction in respect to property used for public purpose, and, where this appears to be the case, there should be no problem in finding that the lessee is subject to the same restrictions that limit the state with respect to the management and operation of the property.[26] The most fundamental consideration in these cases, however, is whether or not the property was operated by the state for a public purpose and whether the lessee continues to operate it for the same general purpose. Thus, if the city leases a public park for operations by a private lessee but the lessee is under a duty to operate it generally as a park, there should not be any substantial problem raised as to the lessee's function as an agency of the state and the lessee's responsibility for observing the Equal Protection Clause.[27] Or the lessee's status as an agent of the city may be determined on the basis of the control that the lessor has retained by the express terms of the lease over the lessee's services and rates. The Supreme Court's recent decision in the *Wilmington Parking Authority* case[28] indicates that the Court will take a close look at lease arrangements where discriminatory practices are alleged. Here, a public off-street parking authority had leased a part of its space for the operation of a private restaurant. Other parts of the parking authority's property had similarly been leased to other persons for carrying on private business. Income from these leases was important to the authority since the revenue from the use of the parking facilities was not in itself enough to meet costs. The leased properties derived their commercial values from the fact that they were part of a parking structure and facility. Moreover, the parking authority had retained substantial controls in the lease, although they did not spell out a duty to serve without discrimination. The lessee operating the restaurant refused to serve Negroes. The Court did not attempt to identify and weigh the various factors that should be taken into account for the purpose of determining whether a lessee of publicly owned property is subject to the Fourteenth Amendment. Stating that the degree of the state's "involvement" was the crucial consideration and emphasizing that the leasing of the properties here was an essential and integral part of the whole public off-street parking enterprise, the Court concluded that under the circumstances of this case the lessee was subject to the Fourteenth Amendment, the same as if it had been incorporated within the lease.[29]

Clearly the Court is feeling its way cautiously in dealing with the lease situation. The Court was careful to limit its holding to the circumstances which presented a strong case for subjecting the lessee to constitutional restrictions.

Closely allied to the lease situation is the case where a state grants financial assistance to a person or organization. Obviously not every person who receives such assistance is to be identified with the state as its agent. It would be fatuous to suggest that the recipient of welfare payments is a state agent in regard to the money so received. The situation is different, however, when a grant of public funds is made to an organization in recognition of the public purpose it serves. Reference may be made, for instance, to grants of financial assistance made by municipalities and counties to libraries which are ostensibly organized and operated under private auspices, but which are open to the public and substantially supported by the public. Here the fact of financial assistance plus the nature of the organization should be sufficient to furnish a finding that the library is subject to Fourteenth Amendment restrictions.[30] The organization's status is analogous to that of the lessee of public property who continues to operate property for essential public purpose.

A private association or group is subject to Fourteenth Amendment restrictions also in the case where the state permits it to perform functions that intrude upon an area of exclusive state responsibility. *Marsh* v. *Alabama*[31] is a striking illustration. Here the Court held that Alabama could not lawfully convict under its trespass statute a Jehovah's Witness who had carried on his religious solicitation and propaganda activities in a town owned by a private lumber company, contrary to the regulations issued by the company's manager. The Court found that this was a violation of the Fourteenth Amendment since the Jehovah's Witness was being deprived of his freedom to carry on his religious activities, a fundamental right protected by the Due Process Clause. Although the state was directly involved because of enforcement of its criminal trespass statute, it appears that the central reason for finding that the state had unconstitutionally deprived the Witness of his religious freedom, even though it was a private company that owned the town and made the rule, was that the town was operated much like a public municipal corporation. The case is not authority for the proposition that the state may not enforce a trespass statute to protect a private homeowner against a trespasser who is distributing religious literature. Here, there was an organized community, the streets were dedicated to a public use, and the community functioned like a city. In effect, the state was permitting a private corporation to exercise important powers and responsibilities in an area of the state's primary authority and responsibility, namely, that of local government, and the action of the local corporation was therefore subject to the same restriction as if it were a public corporation.[32]

Essentially the same theory supported the decision in *Smith* v. *Allwright*,[33] another one of the postwar cases which must be regarded as a very significant one, not only in terms of a dilution of the state action restriction, but also in terms of the effective protection of the Negro's right to vote. Here the Supreme Court held that Negroes could not lawfully be excluded from participation in the Democratic primary in the State of Texas. In prior cases the Court had held that if the exclusion occurred as a result of state law or as a result of grant of authority by state law to the executive committee of the party, this was exclusion by action of state law and was invalid under the Fourteenth and Fifteenth amendments.[34] On the other hand, the Court had held that if the exclusion of Negroes occurred as a result of action by the state convention, this was private action that was not governed by these constitutional restrictions.[35] In *Smith* v. *Allwright*, however, the Court rejected all these distinctions and found that because of the significance of the party primary in the total election process, a process for which the state had to assume total responsibility, the party's action could no longer be characterized as private action. A later decision involving the so-called Jaybird party in Texas pushed the idea still further in finding that a party caucus preceding a primary also was subject to the constitutional rule of nondiscrimination.[36] Similar decisions elsewhere emphasize the idea that, apart from any consideration whether the primary is conclusive in determining the final result, the necessary interrelationship between the primary and the election and the integration of the primary by law into the total election process vest the primary with a public aspect that brings constitutional limitations into play.[37]

Many persons and corporations carrying on business activities of various kinds are subjected to more or less intensive regulation by the state in the exercise of the police power in order to promote the public health, safety, morality, and general welfare. As the scope of the police power is increased in response to new community needs, more and more persons are brought within the reach of regulatory legislation and the purpose of regulation is intensified and broadened. Regulation of this kind is to be distinguished from regulation of persons and companies that receive special grants and franchises and which in a very special way may be deemed to be agencies or instrumentalities of the state. Does the subjection of a person to regulation by the state mean that because his business or other activities are of sufficient public concern to warrant regulation he is therefore so identified with the state or that the state is so involved in his activities that he is subject to Fourteenth Amendment restrictions? The ordinary cases of regulation not requiring the grant of license may be put aside rapidly. The fact alone that a person is subject to law whether it be law in a general way or subject to particular restrictions in dealing with his profession is hardly a basis for saying that the state now assumes responsibility for his action. Should a different result be reached when regulation becomes more intensive and takes the form of the issuance of a license of a person to conduct a particular trade or business? Surely the issuance of a license per se is hardly sufficient to result in characterization of a licensee as an agent of the state. One may note, for instance, the grant of a license to operate a motor vehicle. Obviously this does not have much significance in regard to his status in respect to the state other than that he is a person qualified to drive a car. Likewise, the question may be raised whether the licensing of a plumber or of an electrician in any way affects the status of these persons so far as Fourteenth Amendment restrictions are concerned. These licenses are simply indications by the dispensing authority that these persons have met certain standards imposed by the state in the public interest. They carry no particular value as grants of monopoly as in the case of a certificate of convenience and necessity, and they can be revoked upon showing that the licensee has failed to act in accordance with the statute and regulations.

At this point, mention may be made of the problem, now acute in some of the states, with respect to real estate dealers. If real estate dealers and agents refuse to accept listings that are open to persons of all races or refuse to report offers by persons of a certain race or color, do these discriminatory practices violate the Equal Protection Clause? The question, it should be emphasized, is not whether the state may impose a duty not to discriminate. The question is whether the dealer's position as licensee of the state, conferring authority to engage in real estate transactions, subject to statutory standards, makes him an agent of the state. Absent any grant of monopolistic privilege, it is indeed difficult to see that the position of the real estate dealer is essentially different from that of any other person licensed under state authority. He has no franchise, he has no monopoly, and the issuance of a license simply connotes that he has met the standards prescribed by law. It will take a substantial modification of the state action concept to find that the real estate dealer is subject directly to the restraints of the Fourteenth Amendment.

In concluding this survey of the types of situations in which a private person or group is held subject to constitutional restrictions on the theory that it is serving as an agency or as an instrumentality of the state by discharging a function of the state, reference may be made to the idea occasionally advanced that any action by a private power group should be brought within the coverage of the Fourteenth Amendment. This is on the theory that any group exercising substantial

power over the lives of citizens occupies a place in our pluralistic society that parallels the place of the state.[38]

Thus it has been argued that a large corporation, possessing
vast assets and exercising a substantial influence and control
that affect the future and well-being of many classes of persons and indeed of the entire economic and social community
in which it operates, should be equated with public authority
and governmental power in determining the relevancy of
constitutional restrictions.[39] The fact alone that a group of
persons are incorporated is hardly sufficient to warrant the
conclusion that their action is to be identified with that of
the state. The ease of incorporation under modern laws negates
the idea that the corporate franchise is in itself such a valuable
grant of special public privilege that every corporation must
be viewed as an instrumentality or agency of the state. It is
not the corporate privilege, then, but the large concentration
of economic power in a group, whether incorporated or not,
that becomes the critical element. The results in *Shelley* v.
Kraemer and *Smith* v. *Allwright* are cited to support the idea
that groups representing powerful private controls should be
made subject to constitutional limitations.

This theory has its appeal. The successful functioning of
a pluralistic, democratic society presupposes that all large
power groups shall be subject to controls designed to prevent
an overreaching and abuse of power. But whether this result
should be attained by judicial expansion of the Fourteenth
Amendment to include private action is another question.
This Amendment is directed against the state which under
our system has the monopoly of coercive power. Nothing in
the Supreme Court's opinions lends support to the idea that
the Fourteenth Amendment is relevant unless an organ, agency,
or instrumentality of state government makes itself a party

to denial of equal protection or due process or unless a private person or organization is exercising power in an area of state responsibility. The state or the state's responsibilities must be involved in some way. The state does become involved when a powerful private entity is asserting its rights and privileges in a judicial proceeding, and the fact that a private entity or group enjoys immense powers or monopolistic control is properly taken into account when a court is asked to determine the content and scope of the entity's contractual and property rights and makes its choice between competing interests according to the analysis suggested above. The recognition, however, that powerful private groups may in effect be subjected to constitutional limitations because of the operation of these limitations on the judicial process in the determination of their rights stops short of any general notion that these groups are identifiable with the state and subject to all the same constitutional limitations as the state. If large and powerful private interests are to be subjected to legal restraint and certainly they should be, either in the interest of the general welfare or to prevent abuse and overreaching at the expense of individual liberty, legislation furnishes a more adequate and effective vehicle for imposing such restraint. The federal antitrust and labor statutes and state civil rights and fair employment practice statutes are illustrative of legislation of this kind. Legislation stating general rules applicable to private persons in certain types of situations is better adapted to the solution of these problems than the *ad hoc* process employed by the courts in the interpretation of constitutional limitations.

The Fourteenth Amendment does not on its face reach private action. Private discrimination or private assaults on persons or property or other interferences with the interests of other persons are matters governed by the private law of torts or property, or by criminal law, or by legislation defining new rights and duties. Before the Equal Protection and Due Process clauses can be invoked, it must be demonstrated that the state has in some way made itself a party to the denial of a constitutional liberty. But this distinction between public and private action is not as substantial as might at first appear. Indeed, only a thin wall separates them in some situations. We have in recent years witnessed a development whereby—through the branding of lawless acts by state officers as state action, the expansion of the instrumentality idea, the application of constitutional limitations to private persons exercising power in areas of state responsibility, and the recognition that judicial enforcement of private contract and property rights brings constitutional restrictions into play—progressively greater areas of conduct, at one time deemed private, have been brought under constitutional scrutiny. A notable functional feature of this broadened concept of state action is that it has served an important purpose as part of the total movement for securing equal rights for Negroes. The basic theory of the *Civil Rights Cases* continues unchanged, but the interpretation of this theory in recent decades reveals again that in the field of constitutional law, as in all areas of law, significant developments and changes are obscured by formal adherence to old formulas.

V. CIVIL LIBERTIES:
THE ROLE OF
THE FEDERAL GOVERNMENT

Problems in respect to the recognition and protection of the basic rights of the individual assume a special significance and complexity in a federal system. Whether basic rights as recognized at the national level have a universal or absolute significance in that they serve to limit both the central and the state governments, or whether separate systems of rights are recognized within the federal structure, whether and to what extent the central government may legislate in order to create new rights, and what means are available to the central government for enforcing rights that may be asserted against the states—these are all important phases of the general subject which is described in terms of the role of the federal government with respect to civil liberties.

We are dealing with a subject here of more than academic interest. Probably at no time in our history has the federal government intervened as boldly as in recent years and even during these recent months in order to protect the liberties of the person. Your attention is called to a few of the developments that are relevant to this discussion. Probably the most dramatic and far-reaching development of our generation in the use of federal power to protect civil liberties was the famous decision by the Supreme Court in the school desegregation case and the whole train of events since then designed to make that decree effective. The decision in the *Brown* case[1] and the host of lower court decisions proceeding from it demonstrate the use of the federal judicial power to vindicate the claim of constitutional liberty in the face of adverse state action. In the end, the effective legal enforcement of the desegregation decree rests on the equity power of the federal courts, a subject that will be developed more fully later. The role of the federal government with respect to civil liberties is not limited, however, to the judicial power. You are reminded of current developments which point up other significant phases of this problem. In Montgomery, Alabama, the Attorney General of the United States promptly secured a temporary injunction restraining the Ku Klux Klan and certain named private persons and also certain police officers from interfering with the right of persons to enjoy the facilities of interstate transportation without being subjected to segregation requirements of the local law.[2] The use of federal marshals to enforce this decree, to protect against violence and assure equal protection of the laws, and otherwise to protect federal interests and rights under the Constitution, is a conspicuous illustration of the use of executive power in the area of civil liberties. The Attorney General's effort to intervene in the Prince Edward County, Virginia, school desegregation proceeding in order to compel the county to reopen its schools and to operate them on a nonsegregated basis is premised on an interesting theory as to the standing of the United States in respect to the enforcement of decrees issued by federal courts.[3]

Constitutional Powers of Federal Government Respecting Civil Liberties and Civil Rights

We are here concerned primarily with the power of the federal government through its various organs—namely, the judicial, the legislative, and the executive—to take appropriate steps in regard to the basic rights of the individual as they are allegedly violated by actions of the states or their officers. The further problems respecting the protection of rights against individual aggression will be discussed, however, insofar as they are relevant to the general subject under discussion. This, then, raises a further question about terminology when we speak about civil liberties and the role of the federal government. The term "civil liberties" is here used in a very broad sense to refer to basic rights of the person that are in some way secured to him under the Constitution or the laws of the United States and which are enforceable either against the state or individual persons or both. Admittedly, this is a rather loose definition of civil liberties. The term civil liberties is often used these days in a very narrow way to refer only to a person's right to be free from discrimination based on race, color, religion, or national ancestry. Certainly freedom from discrimination is one important civil liberty, but it hardly embraces the whole area. Others would define the term civil liberties to include not only freedom from discrimination but also the procedural protection of the accused, including the right to a fair trial, and also the freedoms of expression —namely, freedom of speech, freedom of the press, and freedom of religion. This is a more acceptable notion, but even it stops short because if we really want to talk about civil liberties in a constitutional sense, it seems fair to say that the term embraces all the liberties that are recognized and protected under the Constitution including those we have talked about but certainly others as well, including the right to vote, the general freedom embraced by the Due Process Clause of the Fourteenth Amendment, and the freedom from the expropriation of property without compensation.

A distinction that may be observed is that between the term "civil liberties" to characterize liberties or freedoms that may be asserted as against the exercise of governmental power, and the term "civil rights" to connote the rights and privileges that a person may assert against other persons. The whole mass of private rights recognized in the law of torts, contract, and property and protected also by the criminal law, as well as rights created by legislation, fall into this category. My right to be free from bodily assault, to enter into contracts and have them enforced, to keep trespassers off my property are all part of the large mass of civil rights. And if legislation gives me a right to work or a right to be served by a restaurant owner or motel operator, free from discrimination based on race, color, or religion, these, too, fall into the civil rights category. Civil rights are rights created chiefly by common law or statute. Most of the problems discussed in this chapter have to do with civil liberties in the broad sense of constitutional liberties, although it is true that under some constitutional provisions and under some federal legislation civil rights in the narrower sense of this term also come into play.

In any discussion of the role of the federal government with respect to civil liberties two phases of the problem must be kept separate. One is the question of the power to define and formulate the liberty and give content to its meaning. The other is the power to enforce in the sense of the use of appropriate remedial measures in order to make the liberty effective in a practical sense.

The Equal Protection Clause of the Fourteenth Amendment may be used as a concrete example to point up the significance and importance of this distinction. The Fourteenth Amendment says that no state shall deny to any person the equal protection of the laws. What is meant by equal protection, and when does a state deny equal protection of its laws? Obviously the definition of the right here in terms of determining what is meant by equal protection—whether, for instance, it precludes legally sanctioned racial segregation—is a very important threshold question. Who has the final say on this? On the other hand, assuming that equal protection of the law is properly interpreted by the authoritative organ to prohibit racial segregation, what are the practical means of implementing this interpretation and making it operative? At this point we turn to a search for effective remedial devices, including the issuance of restraining orders and injunctions by the federal courts in the exercise of their equity power, the imposition of criminal and civil sanctions as authorized by federal statute, and the use of other possible corrective measures. It is because we must draw this distinction between the definition and formulation of the content of the liberty, on the one hand, and the effective enforcement, on the other, that the problem does assume a certain complexity.

Kinds of Liberties and Rights That May Be Asserted Against States and Individuals—The Distinction Between Protected and Created Rights

Although the major part of this discussion will be centered on the questions relating to the means of enforcement of civil liberties by the federal government as against the states and individuals, this problem cannot be considered in isolation from the initial question of the role of the federal government in defining the content and interpreting the meaning of these liberties. In turning attention at the outset to this latter point, a distinction must be observed between the kinds of liberties or rights that are recognized under the Constitution and which serve as a basis for limitation on either the state governments or individuals, or both.

The first category includes the so-called protected rights or liberties under the Fourteenth Amendment. The Fourteenth Amendment says, "No state shall deprive any person of life, liberty or property without due process of law or deny to any person within its jurisdiction the equal protection of the laws." We have here two categories of liberties or rights: the right to due process of law, and the right to equal protection of the laws. What is important to note here is that the Constitution says that no *state* shall deprive without due process and no *state* shall deny a person the equal protection of its laws. It is for this reason that these are called protected freedoms or rights. They are protected only against the action by the state. This limitation is significant for several reasons as it relates to the role of the federal government in respect to equal protection and due process of law under the Fourteenth Amendment. In the historic *Civil Rights Cases*,[4] discussed in the preceding chapter, the Supreme Court, in holding invalid the civil rights legislation enacted by Congress and designed to secure equal accommodations for Negroes in common carriers, inns, and theaters, said that Congress was not given power under the Fourteenth Amendment to enact positive legislation with respect to civil rights and to secure equality in the enjoyment of rights as against private persons, but that the only power Congress enjoys under the Fourteenth Amendment, as stated in Section 5 of the Amendment, is to enforce these provisions against the states. The enforcement power of Congress is only a corrective power. It follows from this that Congress cannot under the authority of the Fourteenth Amendment enact legislation imposing duties on private persons or defining the content and meaning of due process and equal protection. Determination of the essential content of these terms and of the rights they embrace is reserved for judicial interpretation by the Supreme Court. It is for this reason that these protected rights, the right to due process of law and equal protection of the laws, have really been dependent upon the judicial arm of the federal government for their effective vindication.

What is meant by the due process of law? When does a state deprive a person of life, liberty, or property without due process of law? What is meant by the equal protection of the laws, and when is a law unlawfully discriminatory? All of these questions relating to the primary meaning of the key terms of the Due Process and Equal Protection clauses are questions that have been thrust upon the Supreme Court in its role as final and authoritative interpreter of the meaning of the Constitution. On the other hand, Congress has had a limited role in respect to these protected freedoms since its function is limited to the task of providing ways and means, through concrete remedial measures, for translating into effective enjoyment the rights formulated by the process of judicial interpretation. In other words, it has been the business of Congress, to the extent that it has concerned itself with these matters, to provide various types of sanctions and to make available in the federal courts various types of remedies whereby the rights to equal protection of the laws and to due process of the law are made effective.

The Congressional role in this respect should not be underestimated. We may tend to forget that Congress has made an important contribution to the Supreme Court's paramount role in this area by giving the Court a power to review the decisions of the highest courts of the state dealing with questions involving rights, privileges, and immunities arising under the Constitution, treaties, and laws of the United States. If Congress were to limit the Supreme Court's appellate jurisdiction as has been several times proposed in recent years in order to deny it opportunity to raise questions arising under the Equal Protection Clause of the Fourteenth Amendment, a large part of the effective apparatus for vindication of these protected rights would be impaired or destroyed. Likewise, Congress has made a valuable contribution to enforcement of the Fourteenth Amendment by making such remedial devices as the injunction, habeas corpus, and the declaratory judgment available in the lower federal courts as well as by legislation subjecting state officers and agents to criminal liability and damage actions in cases where their actions have resulted in denial of due process or equal protection. In closing this discussion of protected rights, it is worth noting that the whole development we have had in recent years directed to the end of terminating law-imposed segregation in public schools is attributable entirely to the action of the federal courts. Congress has taken no positive steps to aid in the more effective enforcement of this decree. Depending, in the first instance, upon the Court's authority to interpret the meaning of equal protection and, in the second instance, upon the power of the federal courts to make their decrees effective, the Supreme Court and the lower federal courts have been carefully, slowly, and at times with great difficulty in the face of determined opposition, making their way in the attempt to convert the Court's decision into an operating rule of law throughout the country.

Apart from protected rights, the Constitution and the laws of the United States are a source of other rights that may be claimed by persons either in their relation to the states or in respect to private persons. Here we get into a somewhat more complicated area of discussion. It may be characterized as the area of so-called federally created rights, or more simply federal rights, in the sense that these rights are either created directly by the Constitution or by federal statutes or treaties. The distinctive feature of these created rights—and they include several categories in turn—is that they are in a positive sense created or established by the Constitution or laws of the United States as distinguished from the rights that are protected in the name of due process of law or equal protection of the laws. It can be said that the Constitution did not create due process of law nor the notion of equal protection of laws, but it does secure or protect these rights as against invasion by the states. On the other hand, when we turn to the realm of the so-called created rights, we are talking about rights which in a very real sense are the product of the Constitution and of the laws and treaties of Congress pursuant to it.

Perhaps the simplest illustration of created rights are the rights that are specified in the Constitution itself as having a federal character. The most notable of these is the right to vote for congressmen and senators. According to the Constitution those persons who are eligible electors under state law to vote for the most numerous branch of the state legislature thereby become eligible to vote for congressmen and senators.[5] Here the Constitution takes eligibility under state law as a measuring rod and automatically converts this into a qualification to vote for federal officers, so that every person who under state law is qualified to vote becomes a properly qualified federal elector. This right stems directly from the Constitution and is a right which may be appropriately protected by Congress, even though the basic qualification is still determined by state law, subject, of course, to the limitation that there can be no discrimination upon the basis of race, sex, or any other classification which offends the Equal Protection Clause. Because of the distinctively federal character of this right,[6] Congress may take appropriate steps to protect it against the action of both states and individuals, as well as exercise a power expressly given under the Constitution to regulate the time, place, and manner of so-called federal elections.[7] What Congress has done to date in regard to the voting right, which in many respects looms as the central right as far as freedom from discrimination is concerned, will be more fully discussed later. It is sufficient here to note that Congress has a broader authority in protecting this right than it has with respect to the general right to equal protection and due process of law.

In the second category of so-called created rights are those described as the privileges and immunities of citizens of the United States, such as the right of interstate travel, the right to run for federal office, the right to assemble to discuss federal legislation and to petition Congress for redress of grievances, the right of access to the federal government and its offices, to the enjoyment of protection by its officers and the enjoyment and benefit of the decrees of its courts. This is not the occasion to discuss at length the history of the Privileges and Immunities Clause of the Fourteenth Amendment, or to ask the question whether this clause has received the construction originally intended when the Fourteenth Amendment was adopted, or whether the Court was right in the *Slaughter-House Cases*[8] in giving this clause a narrow construction. The Fourteenth Amendment says that everyone born or naturalized in the United States is a citizen thereof and of the state wherein he resides and then goes on to say that no state shall abridge the privilege and immunities of citizens. In the famous *Slaughter-House Cases* that came before the

Court not so long after the. Fourteenth Amendment was adopted, the Court refused to equate the privileges of citizenship with the so-called common callings or common rights and instead declared that the privileges of citizenship were those peculiar to citizens in our federal structure of government and embraced only the rights peculiar to the relationship between the citizen and the national government and having their source in the existence and powers of the federal government. Thus, the Court in its extensive dicta in the *Slaughter-House Cases* affirmed the idea expressed in the earlier *Crandall* case,[9] that the privilege of interstate travel was a privilege of national citizenship since access of the citizen to the seat of the federal government was an important facet of his relation to this government. On the whole, then, the privileges and immunities of citizenship include only a limited category of freedoms or rights. What is included in this category is a judicial question, but it appears that sanctions for violation of these may be applied both against the state and individuals in view of the fact that these are distinctively federal rights that have their origin in the establishment of the federal system and the creation of the status of federal citizenship.[10]

Finally, the category of federal or federally created rights includes all the rights derived from legislation enacted by Congress in the exercise of its delegated powers and rights arising from treaties to which the United States is a party. Within the areas of its substantive legislative powers, Congress may create rights that are enforceable both against the states and private individuals. Thus, Congress has a sumptuary legislative power over territories of the United States. Its power here is as broad as that of a legislature over a state's territories so far as general legislative power is concerned. The most conspicuous example of a federal territory is the

District of Columbia. Here Congress has complete legislative power and may enact legislation designed to add to the rights which are already secured to persons there by the Bill of Rights. If Congress wants to provide that every person engaged in a public business or calling shall serve everyone without discrimination, it may appropriately do so, and it may impose sanctions, criminal and civil, against private individuals engaged in these callings who fail to comply with the statute.[11] Likewise, Congress may provide with respect to every employer in a territory under Congressional control that he shall not discriminate in his employment practices by reference to race or color and provide for appropriate sanctions in case of violation.

Similarly, under its power to regulate commerce, Congress may legislate for very broad purposes related to civil rights. Thus, Congress has made it unlawful for interstate carriers to discriminate in their service on the basis of race or color or to enforce rules requiring racial segregation.[12] Because of this legislation the Supreme Court held in the recently decided *Boynton* case[13] that a restaurant owner serving passengers engaged in interstate travel may not lawfully deny service to a Negro passenger. The relation of this decision to the later Freedom Riders movement is apparent. Recently Congress has made it illegal to ship in interstate commerce explosives designed to be used for blowing up, dynamiting, or otherwise damaging churches or synagogues.[14] Under the national labor legislation, Congress has created a fundamental statutory right of collective bargaining and corollary rights to strike and picket within the limits recognized by Congress.[15] Attention is also called to recent proposals that Congress make it unlawful for a manufacturer or employer engaged in production for commerce to discriminate in his employment practices on the basis of race, color, or religion. Undoubtedly the principle that sustains the National Labor Relations Act as an appropriate exercise of the power of Congress to regulate commerce would be adequate to sustain this kind of fair employment practice legislation as well. Under the Federal Communications Act,[16] also based on the commerce power, Congress has made it unlawful to tap telephone wires, at least to the extent that the evidence obtained thereby cannot be used in federal courts. Similarly, Congress may act to protect the secrecy and privacy of the mails and of telegraphic communication.

The spending power of Congress is another source of authority to deal with civil rights. The current discussions apropos federal aid to education highlight the possibility of using the federal spending power as a means of promoting state observance of constitutional rights. Thus it has been proposed as a condition to federal spending for public schools that no federal money shall go to aid in the construction or operation of schools that practice racial segregation. Similarly, nondiscriminatory provisions may be included in federal legislation appropriating money in aid of both public and private housing. These are all mentioned at this point simply to indicate that apart from its corrective power to enforce the Due Process and Equal Protection clauses of the Fourteenth Amendment, Congress has substantial reservoirs of power to draw upon to further a program of protecting minorities against discrimination in transportation, employment, education, and housing.

In these areas of its own legislative competence and authority, the federal government has adequate power not only to create rights but to secure their enjoyment by providing sanctions and remedies not only against those who acting under authority of the law may be found to violate these rights but against private persons as well. Indeed, the power to deal with all persons coming directly within the scope of its legislative competence is necessarily central to any discussion of the substantive powers of the federal government. If Congress provides that every employer engaged in production for commerce shall not discriminate on the basis of race or color in the choice or discharge of employees, obviously Congress may choose various means to make this policy effective. It may provide criminal sanctions against employers found guilty of violating the act; it may authorize a damage action against the employer by persons discriminated against; it may authorize an injunctive remedy to enjoin employers from continuing these practices; or it may create an administrative remedy pursuant to which an employer's practice is characterized after a hearing by a board as an unfair labor practice which may be corrected by an appropriate order directed to the employer and violation of which may be made punishable. In other words, when we are dealing with rights created by Congressional legislation in the exercise of the independent substantive powers of Congress, we are talking about rights which in the more accurate and strict sense may be called civil rights since they give rise to reciprocal obligations enforceable against private persons, as distinguished simply from constitutional liberties that are protected against government in the interest of individual freedom.

It has been necessary to present this preliminary picture with respect to kinds and classes of liberties or rights that either receive federal protection or have their source in the Constitution and laws of the United States in order to lay the foundation for a more intensive examination of the role of the federal government in respect to the protection of civil liberties. It should be emphasized again, in the light of the analysis made above, that we have the basic distinction between

the so-called rights that are protected against the states under
the Fourteenth Amendment and, in turn, a body of so-called
created rights, some of which are created directly by the
Constitution, either expressly or by implication, and some of
which are created by Congress. In a case of the protected
rights Congress has a limited function to perform in authorizing corrective devices whereby the judiciary and the executive can make these protected rights effective. In the case
of the federally created rights the courts have an important interpretative and enforcement function, but Congress has a
broad function since it can create rights of this character as
well as prescribe the remedies for making them effective.

Finally, the role of the executive department in respect
to both classes of rights should be noted. Without, at this
point, examining in detail problems that will be discussed
more fully later, it is relevant to point out that the executive
department is charged with the general enforcement of the
laws of the United States as well as with specific functions
committed to it by Congress. An important role of the executive department is to see to it that the independence and
integrity of the federal courts are observed and that judicial
orders are carried out. Another important function is to see
that the basic conditions of peace and order are maintained,
and these, in turn, may involve the protection of important
constitutional rights as will be pointed out later. Moreover,
some remedies that Congress may provide for the vindication
of certain rights depend for their effectiveness upon the ag-
gressiveness, the initiative, and the energy of the executive as
it operates through the Justice Department or otherwise in the
prosecution of these remedies.

The Enforcement Powers and Functions of the
Three Branches of the Federal Government

It is against the background of this analysis of the respective
roles of the various organs of the federal government in regard
to the formulation, interpretation, and enforcement of what
in a broad sense we have described as civil liberties under the
Constitution, and which may be enforced against the states
and in some instances against private individuals, that we take
a closer look at the problems raised particularly in respect to
enforcement since this is the matter of chief current concern.

It is fair to say that the most important question in the field
of equal protection at the present time is the enjoyment of
the right to vote without racial discrimination. It is clear
that every person who meets voting qualifications under state
law is eligible to vote for federal officers as a matter of federal
right. Moreover, a person who otherwise qualifies to vote under
state law cannot be denied the right to vote in either federal
or state and local elections on the basis of race or color without
violation of the Fifteenth Amendment as well as the Fourteenth Amendment's Equal Protection Clause. In this sense
there is no question about these rights. The real problem
centers on the effective enjoyment of these rights. We know
that Negroes are in fact still disenfranchised in a number of
communities. The problem then is to find remedies that will
insure actual enjoyment of the voting privilege. The same
can be said with respect to the right of Negro children to
attend nonsegregated schools. There is no question but that
this right is fully established by the authoritative decision
of the United States Supreme Court in *Brown* v. *Board of
Education*.[17] Yet we do know also that there are still sections
of the country where very little progress has been made. The

practical implementation of this right by means of federal court orders and other remedial devices designed to insure that the Supreme Court's decision will be carried out with all deliberate speed presents the really important and critical aspects of the desegregation problem.

In looking at the questions, particularly those of contemporary interest, we may examine the problem in regard to the three branches of the government, starting again with the judiciary because of the central role that it occupies here.

The point was made earlier that the most potent, drastic, and effective weapon in the hands of the federal judiciary is the equity decree, and certainly events of the last few years fully support this conclusion. It is in the exercise of this equity power that the federal courts have done their most effective work in dealing with the problem of desegregation. If we may judge by developments of just the last few months, it appears that the Justice Department of the United States is intent on an even wider use of the federal equity power as a means of carrying out a more intensive program for protection of civil liberties. The use of the federal equity power to issue restraining orders or injunctions deserves a close look. The injunction is a peculiarly effective and drastic remedy because it can be issued rapidly, because it is flexible and adaptable to different situations, and because it subjects any person guilty of violating it to a summary contempt procedure whereby a person is subject to fine or imprisonment or both without the benefit of a jury trial. Although the equity remedy has its dangers, as pointed up by the widespread use of injunctions at an earlier time in cases of labor disputes, a practice terminated by the Norris-La Guardia Act,[18] the factors that contribute to make it a powerful judicial tool point up its strength and effectiveness as a means available to the federal judiciary for dealing with current problems relating to the protection of civil liberties. It is fair to say that we are at present witnessing the use of federal equity power for the purpose of enforcing equal protection of the laws in a manner reminiscent of its earlier use as a means of dealing with labor disputes, a practice that gave rise to the charge of government by the judiciary. Attention may be called, for instance, to the way in which New Orleans, indeed, the State of Louisiana, at the time of the school crisis there, was blanketed by a series of decrees issued by the federal district court against the Governor, the Attorney-General, a state judge, the Superintendent and School Board of New Orleans, the Orleans Parish School Board, the City of New Orleans, and even the state legislature.[19]

An interesting phase of the use of the injunctive power that has become apparent in recent developments is the transformation of a constitutional limitation from one that is simply a limitation on the states to one that may for all practical purposes reach private persons. The Equal Protection Clause, we know, is a limitation on the states and their agencies. A school board that discriminates against Negro children is an agency of the state, and its discriminatory policy violates the Equal Protection Clause. On the other hand, a private person who discriminates does not come within the Equal Protection Clause. If private persons bring pressures to bear on a Negro parent not to send his child to a desegregated school, this in itself raises no problem under the Equal Protection Clause of the Fourteenth Amendment. But suppose that in a given case a federal court by its decree sanctions a school board's proposal for integration and, pursuant to this, Negro parents send their children to a desegregated school. If at this point private individuals such as employers or neighbors bring pressures to bear on a Negro parent to keep him from sending his child to a school, by threatening loss of job, violence, or similar consequences, these threats may well be found to be an obstruction to the carrying out of the federal court order, and for this reason these persons may be brought by appropriate measures within the range of the federal contempt power. The theory here is not that private persons are subject to the Fourteenth Amendment, but rather that private persons may not interfere with or obstruct the carrying out of the orders of a federal court or interfere with the enjoyment by persons of rights that may be said to have their origin in federal court orders and thereby have become federally created rights.[20] Likewise, any attempt on the part of agitators to arouse a community in opposition to a court order may be reached in the same way. Thus, Mr. Kasper in Tennessee was held in contempt of court because of his efforts in obstruction of a decree.[21]

The current attempt of the Attorney General of the United States in Prince Edward County, Virginia, to intervene in a suit to compel the reopening of the public schools in that area reveals another interesting, if not novel, aspect of reliance on the judicial power in the current battle over desegregation.[22] At the present time the schools, as an alternative to operating on an integrated basis, are not operating at all, with the result that while a number of white children have been going to privately operated schools, the Negro children have, in fact, not been receiving equal education. The theory of the Attorney General in attempting to intervene is that since there was a decision by a federal district court requiring desegregation, the United States has standing now to compel Prince Edward County to carry out that order by affording equal protection to all children in that county, particularly since other counties of the state are continuing to keep their public schools open.

The action of the Attorney General in the Prince Edward County case does point up at once the weakness of relying almost wholly on the judicial power in the course of ordinary litigation for dealing with these questions. The federal judicial power can be exercised only in the course of concrete litigation, that is, in the course of cases or controversies between parties having adverse interests. For this reason the federal judicial power can be invoked only by persons having an appropriate interest, and this means usually an appropriate private interest. In the school desegregation cases, theoretically only Negro parents speaking on behalf of Negro children have standing to bring a suit to compel desegregation. But while Negro parents are the nominal plaintiffs, as a practical matter much of this litigation is initiated and carried on by the National Association for the Advancement of Colored People. But even here, at least in form, the usual theory of private litigation is observed. The Attorney General's action in bringing suit on behalf of the United States to intervene in a federal desegregation proceeding is very significant in that, if successful, it opens up the possibility of a substantially expanded role of the executive department in securing compliance with desegregation orders. Whether or not the Attorney General, absent express statutory authority, will be successful in maintaining standing of the United States in a proceeding like that in Prince Edward County is not at all certain.[23] Certainly it cannot be said that as a general rule the United States is a proper party in interest to bring suits to enforce private rights protected under the Fourteenth Amendment, or that it has standing to intervene in a proceeding to enforce a judicial decree, unless there is express statutory authority to do so or it is demonstrated that enforcement of the decree is being hindered by force and violence.[24]

Finally, it may be observed that at a given point federal judicial power may fail completely by way of effective enforcement where it encounters substantial resistance in the community and the usual processes of enforcement prove ineffective. In Little Rock, Arkansas, because of the obstructive tactics employed by the governor of the state and the encouragement given to persons and groups acting in opposition to the desegregation decree, it was not possible for Negro parents to send their children in safety to the desegregated schools. In view of the inability of the regular officers of the court, the marshals, to enforce the court's decree, intervention by the executive became necessary. President Eisenhower resorted to the use of federal troops solely for the purpose and wholly on the theory that these were necessary to remove obstructions to the carrying out of the decree of a federal court.[25]

We turn now to a closer look at the role of Congress in respect to civil liberties. At this point, in view of the earlier preliminary analysis of Congressional powers in the field, we need to consider only what Congress has done and the problems currently faced with respect to rights, first, that are protected against the states by the Fourteenth Amendment and, secondly, that arise directly from the Constitution or are otherwise included in the privileges of national citizenship.

The legislation that Congress has enacted in order to provide sanctions in case of state violation of the so-called protected rights is a curious potpourri which can be explained only by historical considerations. The provisions of the Federal Civil Rights Act designed to provide both criminal and civil sanctions against those who acting under color of law are responsible for the deprivation of rights protected under the

Constitution of the United States are a patchwork of ambiguous and to some extent obsolete language coupled with poor draftsmanship, and it is surprising, indeed, that the courts have been able to do anything with this legislation at all. Nearly all of this legislation goes back to the time immediately following the Civil War or immediately following the adoption of the Fourteenth Amendment, and some of it is very plainly intended to deal with the Ku Klux Klan. The Supreme Court has attempted to give some meaning to these statutes and in doing so has given them a fairly liberal interpretation. Section 242 of the United States Criminal Code provides for criminal sanctions against persons who acting under color of state law cause the deprivation of any right, privilege, or immunity secured under the constitutional laws of the United States. Under this section a criminal prosecution may be brought against any state officer who acts in a deliberate way to deny equal protection or due process to any person, and, as pointed out in the preceding chapter in connection with the discussion of the "state action" concept, the Supreme Court held in the *Screws* case[26] that a state peace officer could be indicted under this section for causing the death of a prisoner in his custody even if his action was totally lawless and in violation of state law. But the broad and indefinite language of this statute and the technicalities involved in properly instructing a jury under it combine to make it a relatively ineffective statute. Moreover, the difficulty of getting a verdict from a jury drawn from the locale makes it clear that no major or even substantial reliance can be placed upon criminal legislation as a means of putting teeth into the federal enforcement of civil liberties.

Apart from criminal legislation, Congress has also provided civil remedies directed against persons who acting under color of law have caused a deprivation of rights protected under the Constitution.[27] This legislation recently came before the Court in *Monroe v. Pape*.[28] Here, a person whose home had been unlawfully invaded by police officers in an early morning effort to apprehend a criminal brought suit against these officers for invasion of the privacy of his home under the authority of the federal statute. The big question before the Court was whether the defendant peace officers had acted under color of law in making the lawless search and forcing themselves into the home. Admittedly, the officers in making this search had violated state law. In view, however, of the cases interpreting the term "color of law" in the corresponding criminal statute, it was not surprising that the majority of the Court held that these officers had acted under color of law and that the plaintiff, therefore, stated a cause of action for damages.

The civil remedy against the state officer for damages may be pursued more frequently than a criminal prosecution, but even this may be an empty remedy unless a state officer has assets available to satisfy a judgment against him. It would be much more helpful if Congress gave a cause of action against the municipal corporation or the state agency that employs officers who have been guilty of the kind of lawless conduct that results in violation of constitutional rights. In the *Pape* case the attempt was made to hold the City of Chicago as the employing corporation, but the Court, basing its decision on historical intent behind the federal civil rights legislation, found that there was no purpose on the part of Congress to give a cause of action against municipal corporations. Had the Court reached a contrary result, it would have marked the beginning of a new federally developed municipal tort liability predicated on violation of constitutional limitations.

It seems quite clear that unless and until the public agencies and municipal corporations are held liable as employers for the unlawful actions of their employees, the damage action under the federal civil rights legislation will not be a very effective device for enforcing the Fourteenth Amendment.

Attention may be called at this point to proposals introduced in Congress from time to time by way of proposed federal antilynch legislation. It is apparent that the statutory provisions referred to above cannot be the basis of either criminal or civil sanctions against persons who may engage in lawless conduct at the expense of the rights of others but whose actions are not to be identified with the state. For instance, if a group of persons seizes an individual who is accused of a crime and lynches him or subjects him or his property to injury or damage, there is no action under color of law in these cases that would warrant punishment by the federal government, or if a group of persons does damage to a synagogue or dynamites a church, there is not the requisite governmental action or action under color of law to sustain an indictment. It is because of the limitations of the present legislation that various proposals have been made to deal with the lynching situation. Fortunately, lynching in the usual sense has declined substantially in this country and can no longer be said to present a national problem, but periodically so-called antilynch bills continue to be introduced in Congress. They may be narrow in their scope or they may be broad. They may be directed toward lynching that results in the death of a victim with the thought of imposing criminal sanctions either upon the peace officers who permit the lynching or upon the members of the lynching group who are guilty of the offense. Other proposals may go much further. They may even define a lynch assault as any assault on a person or property because of race, color, religion, or national ancestry. The remedies and sanctions take a broad form and may provide for criminal sanctions against police officers who failed to use their best efforts to prevent a lynching assault, criminal sanctions against the persons taking part in the lynch mob, and civil sanctions against the municipality where a lynching took place.

It is apparent that at least some of these proposals raise substantial constitutional questions. It may be assumed that a state peace officer who negligently or culpably fails to exercise his best efforts to protect a prisoner may be subjected to federal sanctions on the theory that here the state has by this culpable inaction permitted a deprivation of life or liberty without due process of law. There seems to be a good case also for permitting a civil action against a municipal corporation or other local unit that permits a lynching to take place on the theory that the Constitution does in the Fourteenth Amendment impose a duty upon the state to use its best efforts to prevent this kind of action and perhaps makes it an insurer against this kind of lawlessness. But it is quite a different matter to provide for criminal sanctions against persons who take part in a lynching mob. It would be a distortion of words to say that they are acting under color of law. The only tenable theory for reaching them is that it is necessary, as Congress has determined, to punish them in order to enforce the state's duty to provide equal protection and to assure due process of law. It is clear that in order to enforce a judicial order directed against a state agency the federal judicial or executive power may be utilized against individuals who interfere with the carrying out of the order.[29] Perhaps it is equally tenable to say that criminal actions may be authorized against private individuals whose actions make it difficult in a given situation for the state to carry out its duty under the Fourteenth Amendment to secure the equal protection of the law for all of its citizens. Surely this means that it must use its powers even-handedly to prevent violence that disturbs the peace at the expense of a certain class of citizens.

The provisions of the Civil Rights Act that furnish some means of protecting either through criminal or civil remedial devices and sanctions the right to due process and equal protection of the laws when violated by the state or those acting under state authority are paralleled by the provisions that furnish a vehicle for the protection of the so-called created rights. Under Section 241 of the Criminal Code, criminal sanctions are directed against two or more persons who conspire to injure any citizen in the free exercise or enjoyment of any rights secured or protected by the Constitution or laws of the United States. This section may be used to punish private persons who are guilty of infraction of rights that may be characterized as federally created rights, including the rights of citizenship. Thus an indictment would lie under this section against persons conspiring to interfere with a citizen's right of interstate travel. But, again, this section, like its parallel Section 242, has its weakness in that it is drafted in a very general way and does not lend itself well to enforcement.

We turn now to federal legislation in the most sensitive area of civil rights, namely, the enjoyment of the right to vote free from discrimination based on race or color. An important distinction must be observed at the outset between the right to vote for congressmen and senators, on the one hand, and for state and local officers on the other. Basically the right to vote for state and local officers is derived from the state constitution and laws and is not a federal right in the same way that the right to vote for congressmen and senators is. The states are free to define their qualifications for voting for state office subject to the limitations imposed by the Constitution under the Fourteenth, Fifteenth, and Nineteenth amendments, namely, there can be no abridgment of the right to vote either because of race or color or because of sex, and furthermore there can be no classification in the voting privilege which violates the Equal Protection Clause of the Fourteenth Amendment. It is apparent from these restrictions that the Constitution prohibits only state action which constitutes an unreasonable discrimination in the granting of the voting privilege or otherwise denies it because of race or sex. In turn, the power of Congress to enforce this right is limited to providing sanctions against state action.

The right to vote for federal officers—namely, congressmen and senators—presents quite a different situation. As pointed out earlier, the right to vote for congressmen and for senators is granted directly by the Constitution and is put into the category of a so-called federally created right. However, this right is conditioned by reference to state law inasmuch as those persons who are qualified to serve as electors of the most numerous branch of the state legislature automatically are made federal electors.[30] This does throw the matter back on state law in the sense that state qualifications must be considered, and, in turn, of course, the validity of the state qualifications may be challenged under the Fourteenth, Fifteenth, and Nineteenth amendments. But the basic right to vote for federal officers is granted by the Constitution, and as long as the qualifications are met, the right to vote may be said to be universal in the sense that Congress has a broad power to protect this right—a much broader power than it has for protecting the right to vote for state officers against unwarranted state discrimination.[31] Congress has two sources of power to legislate in order to protect the right to vote for federal officers. One is the power given under Article 1 to regulate the time, place, and manner of elections. The regulation of the manner of elections implies a power to prescribe punishment and other sanctions for persons whether acting in an official capacity or not who are guilty of intimidation or fraud with respect to the voting process.[32] The other power is the implied power to do what is necessary and proper to secure, strengthen, and protect the right created by the Constitution, and it is probably this implied power which furnishes the basis for the recent legislation on the subject. This implied power is broad enough to reach all persons who in any way interfere with the enjoyment of the federal voting right.[33]

Attention may be directed momentarily to a question which is always sure to arise in any discussion of new proposals by way of federal civil rights legislation, and that is that Congress outlaw the requirement now found in a few states that a person pay a poll tax as a condition to voting. Although bills to this effect are frequently introduced, the power of Congress to do this is subject to serious question. It must be remembered that under the Constitution the states have the power to prescribe qualifications for voting and that the express power of Congress in respect to federal elections has to do with regulating the time, place, and manner of voting. The real question presented here is whether or not the prescription of state law that every person pay his poll tax and present evidence of such payment as a condition to registration for voting is a qualification or whether this is a matter that goes to the power of Congress to regulate the manner of voting. The argument on the latter point is that to require evidence of the payment of the poll tax is to confuse collection of taxes with the voting process and that Congress may appropriately outlaw this so far as voting for federal officers is concerned. In view of the historical power of the states over the subject and the further consideration that payment of taxes has at various times been considered a qualification for voting, it is neither arbitrary nor an undue stretching of the concept to say that requiring payment of a poll tax as demanded by local law is a qualification for voting, and if this is the case, Congress has no power to remove this qualification so long as it is otherwise valid. The Supreme Court has already held that the payment of a poll tax as a condition of voting is not in itself an improper classification under the Equal Protection Clause of the Fourteenth Amendment.[34] In view of these considerations, there is at least serious reason to doubt the constitutionality of federal legislation aimed at elimination of the poll tax, and in any event it must be clear that at most this would be valid only insofar as it related to the right to vote for federal officers.

The more important questions have to do with the right to vote on the part of persons who are otherwise qualified under state law, but who, as a matter of practice, are the victims of discrimination. I refer particularly to the effective disenfranchisement of Negroes. It is safe to say that over the long run the real position of the Negro so far as the enjoyment of rights is concerned will be determined by his effective enjoyment of the voting privilege. This is more significant than whether or not he sends his children to nonsegregated schools, for if the Negro's voice can be made effective politically, it will prove to be the most potent weapon for obtaining the enjoyment of other rights.

The question here is not one of whether the Negro has a right to vote along with others in either federal or state elections. Although state law controls qualifications of voting, under the Fifteenth Amendment no state may prescribe any qualifications that operate to abridge the right to vote because of race or color. Hence, any state law which, on its face, discriminates against Negroes in the voting privilege, whether it be in regard to voting for federal or state officers, is invalid. Moreover, following the decision in *Smith* v. *Allwright*,[35] it is clear also that this right extends not only to vote in the final election, whether it be for federal or state officers, but in primary elections as well, even though it was claimed that these are under the control of private political associations.

We start here then with a constitutional basis of the Negro's right to vote, which theoretically puts him in the same position as the white person—he has a right to be free from discrimination in voting for federal and state officers and this right extends to the primary as well, and any state qualification or other state action which disenfranchises him because of race is unconstitutional.

The real problem, however, is the practical one of converting the paper right to vote into a right enjoyed and exercised in fact. This practical problem presents several aspects. There is the problem, first of all, of working out a remedial device that will insure, as far as possible, the Negro's right to register and to vote notwithstanding obstructive tactics by local registration officers and election officials. Civil and criminal sanctions against local officers responsible for denying the right to vote are not the answer. The Negro's interest is in a specific remedy or arrangement that will enable him to vote, not in a nominal damage remedy. This means bringing local election officials more directly under the immediate supervision and control of federal authorities in some way. The first effective step in this direction was taken with the enactment of the Civil Rights Act of 1957.[36] Probably the most important feature of this legislation was the section which authorized the Attorney General to bring suit on behalf of Negroes in order to enjoin violation of their voting rights.[37] The effect of such a proceeding is to subject registration officials to the risk of a contempt proceeding in the event that they persist in discriminatory practices. Giving authority to the Attorney General to bring such a suit in order to assert the rights of Negroes is in itself an effective step, both because it takes the burden away from individual Negroes or organizations representing them to bring the suits in the first instance and because it may have the effect of relieving Negroes from economic burdens and reprisals that would be effectuated if they themselves brought the suits. In the important *Raines* case[38] the Supreme Court held that, because of the public interest in the enforcement of these rights, Congress could properly authorize a suit like this in the name of the United States. According to Justice Brennan's opinion, "there is the highest public interest in the due observance of the constitutional guarantees, including those that bear most directly on private rights, and we think it perfectly competent for Congress to authorize the United States to be the guardian of that public interest in a suit for injunctive relief."[39]

The use of the criminal contempt power as a means of enforcing an equitable decree affords a means for bypassing the right to jury trial. This was recognized in the Congressional debates over the 1957 act.[40] In deference to the jury trial principle vigorously asserted by the southern bloc in opposition to the use of the equity power to enforce voting rights, the concession was made that if, in the event of a criminal contempt conviction following trial without a jury, a fine imposed exceeded $300 or a jail sentence imposed exceeded 45 days, the party is entitled to a trial *de novo* before a jury.[41]

The other important feature of the 1957 act was the creation of the Civil Rights Commission, the first commission of this kind in the history of the country.[42] The Commission is charged with the task of making studies and investigations of alleged denials of civil rights including voting rights, authorized to conduct hearings, and directed to make reports to Congress and the President. The Commission was clothed with the power of subpoena, and during the first three years of its life it conducted extensive hearings and in 1959 submitted its final report which included, *inter alia*, the recommendation that its life be extended and that further legislation be enacted.[43] As might be expected, the Commission ran into difficulty in conducting its hearings and its power was challenged almost immediately, but to date its authority has been sustained by the Court. The most notable decision concerning the Commission was *Hannah* v. *Larche*,[44] in which the power of the Commission to conduct hearings in order to question witnesses on the basis of information already supplied by secret informers was upheld by the Court. The Court took occasion to define the character of the Civil Rights Commission and said that it was not a judicial body but rather an administrative agency established by Congress with a power of investigation resembling that of a Congressional investigating committee or even a grand jury and that, therefore, witnesses called before it were not entitled as a matter of constitutional right to face accusing informers and to cross-examine them. The effect of this decision was to sustain a broad authority in the Commission to investigate and conduct hearings, to use secret informers in the aid of its process, and, in general, to be free from the constitutional limitations applicable to criminal proceedings. The Court found that the authority of Congress to create this Commission rested on its power to enforce the Fourteenth Amendment.

Despite the added sanctions of the 1957 legislation, Congress had not yet really come to grips with the problem of adequate supervision of the registration process to make the voting right effective. Concern over this problem led to the enactment of the 1960 Civil Rights Act.[45] After extended discussions[46] Congress acted to create a system under which federal district courts are authorized to employ so-called registrars who will assist the federal judges in policing the voting registration system and, in effect, will take over in a limited way the function of determining eligibility to vote once a pattern of racial discrimination has been established.[47] The federal court now assumes a responsibility through the use of its registrars for seeing to it that qualified Negroes are actually registered as eligible voters despite obstructive tactics by local officers. It is too early yet to tell whether this process will be effective or whether, as some critics claim, this procedure will be mired in legal technicalities and time-consuming processes. The registrar device represents a considerable intrusion by the federal government into a process normally under state control, and it is not surprising that its constitutionality was challenged in the course of the Congressional debates. In view, however, of the clear evidence respecting continued discrimination against Negroes in enjoyment of the voting privilege and the express power given to Congress under the Fifteenth Amendment to provide appropriate corrective measures, as well as its broad powers over the federal voting privilege, it would be surprising, indeed, if the registrar scheme were held unconstitutional.

Even if the problem of freedom from official discrimination in voting is solved, a big factor that remains is the element of coercion and intimidation that may be brought by private persons and which operates with a repressive effect on the voting right. The reference here is primarily to economic coercion. We may cite the case of Negro farm tenants who allege that they are threatened with eviction because it is known that they voted in a recent election. This, in the end, may be a much more effective limitation on the voting right than any formal limitations or any discrimination practiced by voting officials. What can be done by Congress with respect to this situation, and what has been done? It is here, again, that the distinction between protection of the right to vote for federal officers and the right to vote for state officers becomes important. So far as state elections are concerned, since the whole power of Congress to enact remedial legislation is limited to enforcing the right to vote free from discrimination under the Equal Protection Clause and the Fifteenth and the Nineteenth amendments, it is open to serious question, in view of the long line of decisions going back to the *Civil Rights Cases*[48] and the view expressed there, whether Congress can do anything more than regulate the conduct of officers to see to it that they do not discriminate, as well as provide criminal and civil remedies directed against those acting under color of law. In short, it does not appear that Congress has the power to punish private persons who employ economic sanctions as a means of discouraging the right to vote for state and local officers or to authorize federal courts to employ their equity process for the express purpose of reaching this private discrimination. This conclusion is subject to a qualification that will be developed later.

On the other hand, in view of the plenary power of Congress to protect the right to vote for federal officers, it appears that it would have the authority to protect this right against private as well as official interference or harassment. Certainly Congress can punish persons guilty of fraud, duress, or intimidation where this is directly related to the physical process of voting for federal officers,[49] and the implied power to take all appropriate measures to protect the federally created right to vote should be adequate to include a power to reach private persons who in fact interfere with this right.[50] Indeed, the provisions of the 1957 Civil Rights Act[51] appear to be broad enough to reach private persons, and the question is presently being litigated whether or not a federal court may enjoin landlords from using their power to evict Negro sharecroppers as a means of intimidating or coercing them in the exercise of their right to register or to vote.[52]

The distinction between the power of Congress to protect the federal voting right against private interference and the state voting right only against state interference is subject to a limitation that arises when a federal court uses its equity power to protect the voting right as against abridgment by state officers. In the case of a federal election, the injunction process can be employed in such a way as to enjoin all interference with the voting right and to bring within the reach of the contempt power, at least after notice and hearing, private persons who attempt to interfere. Likewise, if an injunction is issued against state officers to enjoin them from interfering with the voting right, or to compel the registration of certain persons as voters, any private persons interfering with the effective enforcement of the decree come within the reach of the contempt power.[53] Moreover, there is recent authority to the effect that a federal court may enjoin private persons from interfering with the bona fide and voluntary actions of state officers in attempting to conform local practices to the requirements of equal protection as interpreted by the

Supreme Court.[54] This suggests the possibility of using the federal equity power to restrain private persons from taking any steps designed to interfere with the efforts of local election officers to register voters and permit them to vote in accordance with constitutional requirements, whether in federal or state elections.

Attention has been given up to this point to the respective roles of the judiciary and of Congress in the matter of civil liberties. We conclude this discussion with a look at the role of the executive and more particularly that of the President of the United States, who symbolizes the federal executive power. The executive enters into the picture in a number of ways. In the first place, any criminal actions under Sections 241 and 242 of the Criminal Code are initiated by the Department of Justice. Moreover, with respect to the maintenance of civil actions by way of injunction to enforce the provisions of the 1957 and 1960 Civil Rights acts, the initiative must be taken by the Attorney General to bring the suits. The energy and initiative shown here will determine the effectiveness of these remedies. Finally, as previously noted, the Attorney General is now asserting a right to intervene in cases where federal courts have issued desegregation decrees on the theory that the United States has an interest in securing compliance with the decree.[55] If this theory prevails in the federal courts, it will open up a new opportunity for the federal executive to move directly in an attempt to enforce desegregation decrees. All this is quite apart, of course, from the moral authority that the President may assert in dealing with this problem and also the use of the political powers of his office to induce Congress to enact necessary or desirable new legislation. Finally, some attention must be given to the power of the President to use such force as he deems necessary to secure compliance with federal laws and court decrees when all other efforts fail. President Eisenhower's intervention in the Little Rock situation comes to mind at this point. His action had sound statutory support. The statute authorizes the President to call out the armed forces of the United States if necessary in order to suppress domestic violence in a state if it so hinders the execution of the laws of that state as to result in deprivation of constitutional rights or if it opposes or obstructs the execution of the laws of the United States.[56] Although reliance is ordinarily placed on the federal marshals to enforce court orders, when this fails the President does have an adequate source of power provided he complies with the statute and acts within the statutory framework.

Even more interesting questions were raised by the Attorney General's use of a small army of federal marshals and other federal enforcement agents in connection with the outbreak of violence generated by the arrival of the Freedom Riders at Montgomery, Alabama. This contingent of marshals was assembled and sent to Montgomery with apparently several purposes in mind: (1) to preserve the peace and thereby enforce the state's duty of assuring the equal enjoyment and protection of the laws; (2) to protect and enforce the federal right of interstate travel; (3) to enforce a federal district court's order enjoining police officers, the Ku Klux Klan, and certain named persons from taking any steps to interfere with the Freedom Riders' right of interstate travel.[57]

Clearly President Kennedy in dealing with the Montgomery situation could have relied on the same statute on which President Eisenhower relied in part in the Little Rock crisis. Even without express statutory authority, the President probably has an implied authority derived from his office to use appropriate force for protecting and securing the freedom of interstate travel and other national interests.[58]

Whether the Attorney General can assemble and call upon a small army of federal marshals to achieve the same purposes as the President can on the basis of either the President's statutory authority or the inherent authority of his office is by no means clear. The statute refers to the President and does not expressly authorize a delegation of power by him to any other officer. Certainly it would not be argued that the Attorney General has the authority under the statute to call out troops or militia even if power were expressly delegated to him by the President.[59] Moreover, there is nothing to indicate that the President either delegated his statutory or inherent authority to deal with this problem to the Attorney General or issued a formal order which required execution by the Attorney General.[60] The latter's authority to use marshals and other federal law-enforcement officers in the Montgomery situation must, therefore, rest on a different basis unless a theory of implied delegation of Presidential authority can be sustained. An adequate alternative basis does suggest itself. The Attorney General by statute is the administrative officer responsible for directing the work of federal marshals who by statute are given all the powers that sheriffs have under local law.[61] In this capacity it appears that he can mobilize marshals and direct their use both for the general purpose of enforcing federal laws and protecting the federal rights of citizens and also to enforce the decrees of federal courts and remove obstructions to the compliance with these decrees. Certainly it is true that as a matter of political strategy and public psychology it is better to meet these situations if at all possible by using peace officers rather than by using military force.

Quite apart from the drastic use of force as represented by the use of troops or a small army of marshals and federal enforcement officers, it is clear that the President through the Justice Department and also by the general authority of his office can take an aggressive position with respect to the protection of civil liberties. It is clear also that Congress has a potentially large role to perform, and to place the great burden of the job upon the courts is, indeed, to make too great a demand upon one organ of the government. It appears, for instance, that with respect to the enforcement of the desegregation decree, some more rapid progress might be made if Congress were to authorize the use of more flexible devices and administrative arrangements, as in the case of the voting privilege. The judicial process is slow, it is in many respects cumbersome, it operates within the framework of a case or controversy, and it may be questioned whether over the long run the desegregation decree, any more than the right to vote without discrimination, will be carried forward effectively without an effective administrative device for implementing the court's decree. In any event it appears that the intervention of both the executive and Congress in devising new patterns and methods for solving integration problems will be a step forward and will lighten the load of the federal judiciary.

This study has demonstrated that within the limits and framework of our constitutional federal structure there are adequate repositories of power within the federal government for insuring respect and observance by the states of basic constitutional liberties as well as for defining and enforcing a substantial body of civil rights assertible against private persons. All three departments of the federal government have important roles to perform in the discharge of this responsibility. Up to this point the courts have shouldered the greater part of the task, and the executive has come in for second-highest honors. Congress has responded least effectively, and this for political reasons that we can well understand. For over three quarters of a century Congress did nothing in the civil rights field. By enactment of the 1957 and 1960 Civil Rights acts it made important contributions to the practical implementation of the right to vote. Important other tasks remain to be done. The general body of civil rights legislation going back to the Reconstruction period cries out for badly needed revision and modernization. The problems raised by resistance to the Supreme Court's school desegregation decree and the slow movement toward integration in a number of the states make clear also that Congress should use the powers available to it both for encouraging states to comply with the decree and for strengthening the hand of the judiciary and the executive department in dealing with the problem. Moreover, Congress has a larger reservoir of substantive legislative powers it may tap, if it will, in order to enlarge the body of civil rights on the federal level. If Congress defaults in these tasks or fails to exercise its powers, this failure is attributable not to the lack of adequate constitutional power under our federal system but to a system of practical politics in which sectional differences continue to play a large part.

NOTES

NOTES TO CHAPTER I

1. For the President's message to Congress offering his program on school aid, see N. Y. *Times*, Feb. 21, 1961, p. 22. (All references in the footnotes in this book to the New York *Times* are to the City Edition.)

2. See N. Y. *Times*, March 3, 1961, p. 1; March 15, 1961, pp. 1 and 26; March 30, 1961, p. 16.

3. See N. Y. *Times*, Feb. 21, 1961, p. 22; March 9, 1961, pp. 1 and 16.

4. Torcaso v. Watkins, 367 U.S. 488 (1961).

5. McGowan v. Maryland, 366 U.S. 420 (1961); Two Guys from Harrison-Allentown, Inc. v. McGinley, 366 U.S. 582 (1961); Braunfeld v. Brown, 366 U.S. 599 (1961); Gallagher v. Crown Kosher Super Market of Massachusetts, Inc., 366 U.S. 617 (1961).

6. See Everson v. Board of Education, 330 U.S. 1 (1947).

7. *Ibid.*

8. See, e.g., Cantwell v. Connecticut, 310 U.S. 296 (1940); Murdock v. Pennsylvania, 319 U.S. 105 (1943); Kunz v. New York, 340 U.S. 290 (1951); West Virginia State Board of Education v. Barnette, 319 U.S. 624 (1943).

9. See Everson v. Board of Education, 330 U.S. 1 (1947); Zorach v. Clauson, 343 U.S. 306, 312 (1952).

10. 330 U.S. 1 (1947).

11. *Ibid.*, pp. 15-16.

12. Torcaso v. Watkins, 367 U.S. 488 (1961).

13. See I. Stokes, *Church and State in the United States* (1950), 537-39; Pfeffer, "Church and State: Something Less than Separation," 19 *U. of Chi. L. Rev.* 1 (1951); Katz, "Freedom of Religion and State Neutrality," 20 *U. of Chi. L. Rev.* 426 (1953).

14. McCollum v. Board of Education, 333 U.S. 203 (1948).

15. Zorach v. Clauson, 343 U.S. 306 (1952).
16. *Ibid.*, pp. 312-14.
17. McGowan v. Maryland, 366 U.S. 420 (1961); Two Guys from Harrison-Allentown, Inc. v. McGinley, 366 U.S. 582 (1961); Braunfeld v. Brown, 366 U.S. 599 (1961); Gallagher v. Crown Kosher Super Market of Massachusetts, Inc., 366 U.S. 617 (1961).
18. McGowan v. Maryland, 366 U.S. 420 (1961).
19. 366 U.S. 420, pp. 465-67 (1961).
20. 366 U.S. 420, p. 576 (1961).
21. See Hesseltine, *Ulysses S. Grant* (New York: Frederick Ungar Publishing Co., 1935), p. 305.
22. Poe v. Ullman, Doe v. Ullman, Buxton v. Ullman, 367 U.S. 497 (1961). The chief opinion was written by Justice Frankfurter and joined by the Chief Justice and by Justices Clark and Whittaker. Justice Brennan wrote a separate opinion in which he concurred in the determination that these cases presented no real and substantial controversy. Justices Douglas and Harlan dissented in separate opinions. Finding justiciable issues in the cases before them and passing to the merits of the question, they concluded that the statute was unconstitutional. Justices Black and Stewart dissented on the dismissal of the case but did not express conclusions on the meritorious question.
23. Justices Douglas and Harlan. See note 22, *supra.*
24. See Doremus v. Board of Education, 342 U.S. 429 (1952).
25. *Sub. nom.* Massachusetts v. Mellon, 262 U.S. 447 (1923).
26. Kunz v. New York, 340 U.S. 290 (1951); Niemotko v. Maryland, 340 U.S. 268 (1951).
27. 42 U.S.C.A., secs. 291 *et. seq.*
28. See Bradfield v. Roberts, 175 U.S. 291 (1899), where the Court upheld an appropriation of money by Congress to a hospital in the District of Columbia, even though the hospital was owned and operated by an incorporated sisterhood of the Roman Catholic church.
29. In Schemp v. School District of Abington Township, 177 F. Supp. 398 (E. D. Pa. 1959), the three-judge district court held unconstitutional daily Bible reading in the public school as required by

a Pennsylvania statute as well as the practice of saying the Lord's Prayer in unison. Appeal to the Supreme Court was dismissed and the district court's judgment vacated as the result of enactment of a new statute while the appeal was pending. School District of Abington Township v. Schemp, 364 U.S. 299 (1960).

The New York Court of Appeals has recently held constitutional the practice of opening the public school day with the nonsectarian prayer recommended by the Board of Regents. Engel v. Vitale, 10 N.Y. 2d 174, 176 N.E. 2d 579 (1961).

30. See Doremus v. Board of Education, 342 U.S. 429 (1952), holding that a taxpayer as such did not have standing to challenge the validity of a statute requiring the reading of the Bible at the beginning of each school day.

31. Zorach v. Clauson, 343 U.S. 306 (1952).

32. See McLean and Kimber, *The Teaching of Religion in State Universities* (Office of Religious Affairs, The University of Michigan, 1960).

33. See Kauper, "Law and Public Opinion," in *Religion and the State University* (E.A. Walter, ed.; Univ. of Mich. Press, 1958), pp. 69-86.

34. For the essential features and objectives of President Kennedy's program for use of federal funds in aid of education, see his message to Congress on the subject, N.Y. *Times*, Feb. 21, 1961.

35. See N.Y. *Times*, Feb. 21, 1961, p. 22; March 9, 1961, pp. 1 and 16.

36. See N. Y. *Times*, March 3, 1961, p. 1; March 15, 1961, pp. 1 and 26; March 30, 1961, p. 16.

37. Federal expenditures to aid training in science and mathematics find a specific justification in the power to promote the national defense.

38. It is now recognized that Congress has an independent, substantive power to spend federal funds in order to promote "the general welfare." United States v. Butler, 297 U.S. 1 (1936); Steward Machine Co. v. Davis, 301 U.S. 548 (1937).

39. See Everson v. Board of Education, 330 U.S. 1 (1947), holding that use of state tax funds to reimburse parents for the cost of

sending children to parochial as well as public schools was for a proper "public purpose."

40. Pierce v. Society of Sisters, 268 U.S. 510 (1925).

41. Everson v. Board of Education, 330 U.S. 1 (1947).

42. Cochran v. Louisiana Board of Education, 281 U.S. 370 (1930).

43. School Lunch Act of 1946, 42 U.S.C.A., secs. 1751 *et. seq.*

44. 20 U.S.C.A., secs. 401 *et. seq.*

45. The statute expressly authorizes low-interest loans to nonprofit private schools for these purposes.

46. The Vermont Supreme Court in a recent decision held that it was a violation of the First Amendment's nonestablishment clause for a school board to pay tuition charges for a student attending a Catholic high school outside the school district. The school district did not operate a high school, and its practice was to pay the tuition cost of its resident students who attended a high school in another district. Swart v. Smith Burlington Town School District, 167 A. 2d 514 (1961). The United States Supreme Court denied review of the case. Anderson v. Swart, 366 U.S. 925 (1961).

47. Particularly if federal grants were limited to the purpose of constructing facilities for such secular purposes as physical education, science, mathematics, and foreign languages.

48. Under authority of Title IV of the Housing Act of 1950, 12 U.S.C.A., secs. 1749 *et. seq.*

49. See Memorandum on the Impact of the First Amendment to the Constitution upon Federal Aid to Education by the General Counsel of the Department of Health, Education, and Welfare, included in Senate Document No. 29, 87th Cong., 1st Sess., pp. 5 and 24-26.

NOTES TO CHAPTER II

1. 283 U.S. 697 (1931).

2. Cases containing statements either to the effect that the First Amendment freedoms are incorporated in the Fourteenth Amendment or that the effect of the Fourteenth Amendment is to make the First Amendment applicable to the states are collected in Justice Black's separate opinion in Speiser v. Randall, 357 U.S. 513, 530 (1958). There is, of course, a substantial difference

between saying that the First Amendment freedoms are incorporated in the Fourteenth Amendment since they are fundamental freedoms and saying that the First Amendment is made applicable to the states through the Fourteenth.

3. See Justice Black's dissenting opinion in Adamson v. California, 332 U.S. 46 (1947), and Justice Douglas' dissenting opinion in Poe v. Ullman, 367 U.S. 497 (1961).

4. Justice Brennan in his opinion in Ohio *ex. rel.* Eaton v. Price, 364 U.S. 263 (1960), states that whenever freedoms catalogued in the Bill of Rights are recognized as fundamental under the Due Process Clause of the Fourteenth Amendment, they enjoy the same degree of protection as they do under the Bill of Rights. But compare the view expressed in Justice Jackson's dissenting opinion in Beauharnais v. Illinois, 343 U.S. 250 (1952), and in Justice Harlan's dissenting opinion in Roth v. United States, 354 U.S. 476 (1957), and in his separate opinion in Smith v. California, 361 U.S. 147 (1960), that a distinction should be observed between freedom of the press protected under the First Amendment and freedom of the press as a fundamental right protected under the Due Process Clause of the Fourteenth Amendment.

5. See dissenting opinions of Justices Black and Douglas in Dennis v. United States, 341 U.S. 494 (1951), and in Scales v. United States, 367 U.S. 203 (1961); also Justice Black's dissenting opinion in Konigsberg v. State Bar of California, 366 U.S. 36 (1961).

6. Grosjean v. American Press Co., 297 U.S. 233 (1936).

7. Bridges v. California, 314 U.S. 252 (1941); Pennekamp v. Florida, 328 U.S. 331 (1946); Craig v. Harney, 331 U.S. 367 (1947).

8. 303 U.S. 444 (1938).

9. Schneider v. Town of Irvington, 308 U.S. 147 (1939), and other cases handed down at the same time under this same title.

10. Breard v. City of Alexandria, La., 341 U.S. 622 (1951).

11. Martin v. City of Struthers, 319 U.S. 141 (1943).

12. Thornhill v. Alabama, 310 U.S. 88 (1940).

13. See, e.g., Giboney v. Empire Storage and Ice Co., 336 U.S. 490

(1949); Hughes v. Superior Court of California, 339 U.S. 460 (1950).

14. 343 U.S. 250 (1952).

15. See Chaplinsky v. New Hampshire, 315 U.S. 568 (1942).

16. See the opinions for the majority by Justice Harlan in Barenblatt v. United States, 360 U.S. 109 (1959), and in Konigsberg v. State Bar of California, 366 U.S. 36 (1961).

17. Near v. Minnesota, 283 U.S. 697 (1931).

18. *Ibid.*, p. 713.

19. 18 U.S.C.A., secs. 1461-64.

20. 333 U.S. 507 (1948).

21. 352 U.S. 380 (1957).

22. Roth v. United States, Alberts v. California, 354 U.S. 476 (1957).

23. *Ibid.*, pp. 484-85.

24. (1868) L. R. 3 Q. B. 360.

25. The early leading cases are United States v. Kennerley, 209 F. 119 (S. D. N. Y. 1913); United States v. One Book Called "Ulysses," 5 F. Supp. 182 (S. D. N. Y. 1933).

26. See, e.g., Commonwealth v. Isenstadt, 318 Mass. 543 (1945).

27. Commonwealth v. Gordon, 66 D. and C. 101 (Pa. C. P. 1949).

For an excellent treatment of the law of obscenity as it had developed in the federal and state courts prior to the Roth and Alberts decisions, see Lockhart and McClure, "Literature, the Law of Obscenity, and the Constitution," 38 *Minn. L. Rev.* 295 (1954).

28. Roth v. United States, Alberts v. California, 354 U.S. 476 at p. 489 (1957).

For critical discussions of the standard stated by the Court, see Kalven, "The Metaphysics of the Law of Obscenity," 1 *The Supreme Court Review* 1 (1960); Lockhart and McClure, "Censorship of Obscenity: The Developing Constitutional Standards," 45 *Minn. L. Rev.* 5 (1960).

29. People v. Richmond County News, Inc., 175 N.E. 2d 681 at 686 (1961).

30. Kingsley International Pictures Corp. v. Regents of the University of the State of New York, 360 U.S. 684 (1959).

31. The decision and opinions in the Kingsley International Pictures

case, together with the Supreme Court's action in three per curiam decisions, citing Roth and reversing findings below that material was obscene, suggest that the Supreme Court will limit the obscenity concept in a very narrow way and confine it to the so-called hard-core pornography. See Lockhart and McClure, "Censorship of Obscenity: The Developing Constitutional Standard," 45 *Minn. L. Rev.* 5 at pp. 32-39 (1960); also, same authors, "Obscenity Censorship: The Constitutional Issue—What Is Obscene?" 7 *Utah L. Rev.* 289 (1961).

32. Kingsley Books, Inc. v. Brown, 354 U.S. 436 (1957).

33. Smith v. California, 361 U.S. 147 (1960).

34. See New American Library of World Literature, Inc. v. Allen, 114 F. Supp. 823 (N.D. Ohio 1953); Bantam Books, Inc. v. Melko, 25 N.J. Super. 292 (Ch. 1953), modified per curiam, 14 N.J. 524 (1954); H.M.H. Publishing Co. v. Garrett, 151 F. Supp. 903 (N.D. Ind. 1957). See also Note, "Extralegal Censorship of Literature," 33 *N.Y.U. L. Rev.* 990 (1958).

The Supreme Court's recent decision in Marcus v. Search Warrants of Property at 104 E. Tenth St., Kansas City, Mo., 367 U.S. 717 (1961), has some relevancy on this point. Here the Court held invalid on due process grounds a state procedure whereby police officers, pursuant to a broad search warrant, were vested with a wide discretion in making a mass seizure of materials which they determined to be obscene. The seizure was preliminary to a judicial hearing under the obscenity statute. See note 47*a*.

35. Mutual Film Corporation v. Industrial Commission, 236 U.S. 230 (1915).

36. Joseph Burstyn, Inc. v. Wilson, 343 U.S. 495 (1952).

37. Gelling v. Texas, 343 U.S. 960 (1952).

38. Superior Films, Inc. v. Dept. of Education of Ohio, Division of Censorship, 346 U.S. 587 (1954).

39. Commercial Pictures Corp. v. Regents of University of State of New York, 346 U.S. 587 (1954).

40. Holmby Productions, Inc. v. Vaughn, 350 U.S. 870 (1955).

41. Times Film Corp. v. City of Chicago, 355 U.S. 35 (1957).

42. 360 U.S. 684 (1959).

43. Times Film Corp. v. City of Chicago, 365 U.S. 43 (1961).

44. 283 U.S. 697 (1931).

45. Times Film Corp. v. City of Chicago, 365 U.S. 43 at p. 50 (1961).

46. 303 U.S. 444 (1938).

47. This decision points up again the problems arising from the Court's equating of the Due Process Clause of the Fourteenth Amendment with the First Amendment. The effect in a given type of situation may be to weaken the First Amendment by reference to due process considerations rather than elevate due process by the standards of the First Amendment. An alternative consideration suggested by the decision is that free speech and free press occupy a so-called preferred position under the First Amendment only when they relate to matters of political concern.

47a. That the Court will not sanction advance censorship of books is indicated by its later decision in Marcus v. Search Warrants of Property at 104 E. Tenth St., Kansas City, Mo., 367 U.S. 717 (1961), holding invalid on due process grounds a state procedure which permitted police officers, pursuant to a broad search warrant, to exercise a wide discretion in making a mass seizure of printed materials which the police determined to be obscene. See the earlier reference to this case in note 34.

48. Kingsley Books, Inc. v. Brown, 354 U.S. 436 (1957).

49. Chief Justice Warren and Justices Black and Douglas. Although Justice Brennan was one of the four dissenters in the Kingsley Books case, his dissent was on the ground that the New York statute did not give a right of jury trial on the question whether the book was obscene.

50. See the suggestion by Nimmer in his article, "The Constitutionality of Official Censorship of Motion Pictures," 25 *U. of Chi. L. Rev.* 626 at p. 654 (1958), that conduct not be regarded as "obscene" for the purpose of movie censorship unless it constitutes "indecent exposure."

NOTES TO CHAPTER III

1. 367 U.S. 1 (1961).

2. Enforcement of this and other provisions was stayed by Justice Frankfurter pending a decision by the Court at its next term on

the Communist party's motion for a rehearing of the case. See N.Y. *Times,* June 24, 1961, p. 5.

3. 367 U.S. 203 (1961).
4. Dennis v. United States, 341 U.S. 494 (1951); Yates v. United States, 354 U.S. 298 (1957).
5. 365 U.S. 399 (1961).
6. Barenblatt v. United States, 360 U.S. 109 (1959).
7. 366 U.S. 36 (1961).
8. This was the second time the Konigsberg case was before the Court. In the earlier proceeding the Court had held that on the basis of the evidence in the record there was no ground for rejecting the petitioner's application for admission to the bar. Konigsberg v. State Bar of California, 353 U.S. 252 (1957). But the question whether an applicant could be required to answer questions respecting Communist affiliation was not squarely raised in the earlier proceeding.
9. 366 U.S. 293 (1961).
10. See Garner v. Board of Public Works, 341 U.S. 716 (1951); Beilan v. Board of Education, 357 U.S. 399 (1958).
11. Garner v. Board of Public Works, 341 U.S. 716 (1951); American Communications Assn., CIO v. Douds, 399 U.S. 382 (1950).
12. Shelton v. Tucker, 364 U.S. 479 (1960).
13. People of New York *ex rel.* Bryant v. Zimmerman, 278 U.S. 63 (1928).
14. 357 U.S. 449 (1958).
15. 361 U.S. 516 (1960).
16. 364 U.S. 479 (1960).
17. See National Labor Relations Board v. Jones and Laughlin Steel Corp., 301 U.S. 1 at p. 33 (1937).
18. See United States v. Harriss, 347 U.S. 612 (1954), a case arising under the Federal Regulation of Lobbying Act, and United States v. C.I.O., 335 U.S. 106 (1948), and United States v. International Union United Automobile, etc. Workers of America, 352 U.S. 567 (1957), both arising under the provision of the Corrupt Practices Act forbidding political expenditures by corporations and labor unions.
19. International Association of Machinists v. Street, 367 U.S. 740 (1961); Lathrop v. Donohue, 367 U.S. 820 (1961).

20. International Association of Machinists v. Street, 367 U.S. 740 (1961).
21. Lathrop v. Donohue, 367 U.S. 820 (1961).
22. Communist Party of the United States v. Subversive Activities Control Board, 367 U.S. 1 (1961).
23. Wilkinson v. United States, 365 U.S. 399 (1961); Braden v. United States, 365 U.S. 431 (1961).
24. Konigsberg v. State Bar of California, 366 U.S. 36 (1961); *In re* Anastaplo, 366 U.S. 82 (1961).
25. Dennis v. United States, 341 U.S. 494 (1951); Yates v. United States, 354 U.S. 298 (1957).
26. Scales v. United States, 367 U.S. 203 (1961).
27. American Communications Assn., C.I.O. v. Douds, 339 U.S. 382 (1950).
28. Communist Party of the United States v. Subversive Activities Control Board, 367 U.S. 1 (1961).
29. Dennis v. United States, 341 U.S. 494 (1951).
30. Yates v. United States, 354 U.S. 298 (1957).
31. *Ibid.*, p. 321.
32. Scales v. United States, 367 U.S. 203 (1961).
33. See, e.g., their dissenting opinions in Dennis v. United States, 341 U.S. 494 (1951), and in Scales v. United States, 367 U.S. 203 (1961).
34. See dissenting opinion by Justice Holmes in Gitlow v. New York, 268 U.S. 652 (1925), and the concurring opinion by Justice Brandeis in Whitney v. California, 274 U.S. 357 (1927).
35. Barenblatt v. United States, 360 U.S. 109 (1959); Wilkinson v. United States, 365 U.S. 399 (1961).
36. Konigsberg v. State Bar of California, 366 U.S. 36 (1961); *In re* Anastaplo, 366 U.S. 82 (1961).
37. See, e.g., Justice Black's dissenting opinions in Barenblatt v. United States, 360 U.S. 109 (1959), and in Konigsberg v. State Bar of California, 366 U.S. 36 (1961), and the dissenting opinions of both Justices Black and Douglas in Scales v. United States, 367 U.S. 203 (1961). For a complete statement of Justice Black's position, see his lecture, "The Bill of Rights," 35 *N.Y.U. L. Rev.* 865 (1960).

For writings in support of the Black-Douglas thesis, see Meiklejohn, *Political Freedom* (New York: Harper and Brothers, 1960); Black, *The People and the Court* (New York: Macmillan Co., 1960).

38. See his opinions in Dennis v. United States, 341 U.S. 494 (1951); Harisiades v. Shaughnessy, 342 U.S. 580 (1952).

39. Probably the best statement of the theory appears in Justice Harlan's opinion in Konigsberg v. State Bar of California, 366 U.S. 36 (1961).

40. See the references cited in note 37, *supra*.

41. Roth v. United States, Alberts v. California, 354 U.S. 476 (1957).

42. Reynolds v. United States, 98 U.S. 145 (1879).

43. Prince v. Massachusetts, 321 U.S. 158 (1944).

44. Braunfeld v. Brown, 366 U.S. 599 (1961); Gallagher v. Crown Kosher Super Market of Massachusetts, Inc., 366 U.S. 617 (1961).

45. See, for instance, United States v. Oregon, 366 U.S. 643 (1961), where the Court, speaking through Justice Black, held that pursuant to a federal statute the personal property of a veteran who died in a federal hospital was vested in the United States. The Court stated that the statute was a "necessary and proper" means of effectuating the military power of Congress. Two justices dissented on the ground that the federal government did not have jurisdiction over probate matters.

46. Southern Pacific Co. v. Arizona, 325 U.S. 761 (1945).

47. Village of Euclid v. Ambler Realty Co., 272 U.S. 365 (1926).

48. In this connection see Justice Black's dissenting opinion in United States v. Causby, 328 U.S. 256 (1946), and the policy considerations he advances to support his conclusion that the impairment of property interests resulting from the operation of military aircraft should not be considered a "taking" of property.

49. Communist Party of the United States v. Subversive Activities Control Board, 367 U.S. 1 (1961).

50. Barenblatt v. United States, 360 U.S. 109 (1959).

51. Yates v. United States, 354 U.S. 298 (1957); Scales v. United States, 367 U.S. 203 (1961).

52. McCloskey, *The American Supreme Court* (Chicago: University of Chicago Press, 1960), p. 229.

NOTES TO CHAPTER IV

1. For helpful current discussions of the subject, see Abernathy, "Expansion of the State Action Concept under the Fourteenth Amendment," 43 *Corn L.Q.* 375 (1958); Lewis, "The Meaning of State Action," 60 *Col. L. Rev.* 1083 (1960); St. Antoine, "Color Blindness but Not Myopia: A New Look at State Action, Equal Protection, and 'Private' Racial Discrimination," 59 *Mich. L. Rev.* 993 (1961).
2. 4 Wheaton 316 (1819).
3. 109 U.S. 3 (1883).
4. 118 U.S. 356 (1886).
5. See, e.g., Norris v. Alabama, 294 U.S. 587 (1935); Hill v. Texas, 316 U.S. 400 (1942); Patton v. Mississippi, 332 U.S. 463 (1947).
6. Pennsylvania v. Board of Directors of City Trusts of the City of Philadelphia, 350 U.S. 230 (1957).
7. *In re* Girard College Trusteeship, 391 Pa. 434 (1958), cert. denied, Pennsylvania v. Board of Directors of City Trusts of City of Philadelphia, 357 U.S. 570 (1958).
8. Screws v. United States, 325 U.S. 91 (1945).
9. 365 U.S. 167 (1961).
10. *Ibid.*, pp. 171-72.
11. United States v. Classic, 313 U.S. 299 (1941).
12. Cited note 8, *supra.*
13. Ex parte Virginia, 100 U.S. 339 (1880).
14. 365 U.S. 715 (1961).
15. In a series of decisions the Supreme Court invalidated state court decrees enjoining peaceful picketing in enforcement of the state's common law policy, where the decrees were found to violate the constitutional right to freedom of discussion. See, e.g., American Federation of Labor v. Swing, 312 U.S. 321 (1941).
16. 334 U.S. 1 (1948).
17. *Ibid.*, p. 20.
18. Rice v. Sioux City Memorial Park Cemetery, 245 Iowa 147 (1953).

19. Rice v. Sioux City Memorial Park Cemetery, 348 U.S. 880 (1954). Thereafter the Court vacated its judgment and dismissed the writ of certiorari as having been improvidently granted: 349 U.S. 70 (1955).

20. 351 U. S. 292 (1956).

21. See Justice Stewart's separate opinion in Burton v. Wilmington Parking Authority, 365 U.S. 715 (1961).

22. Boynton v. Virginia, 364 U.S. 454 (1960).

23. 49 U.S.C.A., sec. 316 (d).

24. 109 U.S. 3 (1883).

25. Dorsey v. Stuyvesant Town Corp., 299 N.Y. 512 (1949), cert. denied, 339 U.S. 981 (1950).

26. See Lawrence v. Hancock, 76 F. Supp. 1004 (S.D. W. Va. 1948).

27. See Tate v. Department of Conservation and Development, 133 F. Supp. 53 (E.D. Va. 1955), aff'd. 231 F. 2d 615 (4th Cir. 1956), cert. denied, 352 U.S. 838 (1956).

28. Burton v. Wilmington Parking Authority, 365 U.S. 715 (1961).

29. The same result had been reached in Derrington v. Plummer, 240 F. 2d 922 (5th Cir. 1957), where space had been leased for a lunchroom in a county courthouse.

30. See Kerr v. Enoch Pratt Free Public Library, 149 F. 2d 212 (4th Cir. 1945), and compare Norris v. Mayor & City Council of Baltimore, 78 F. Supp. 451 (D. Md. 1948).

31. 326 U.S. 501 (1946).

32. The New York and Virginia courts have distinguished Marsh v. Alabama in cases involving the exclusion of Jehovah's Witnesses from entering large apartment houses, pursuant to general rules against visitors or solicitors, on the ground that in the Marsh case the private corporation was asserting a much wider control, including control of the streets. See Watchtower Bible, etc. Society v. Metropolitan Life Insurance Co., 297 N.Y. 339 (1948), cert. denied, 335 U.S. 886 (1948); Hall v. Commonwealth of Virginia, 188 Va. 72 (1948), appeal dismissed, 335 U.S. 875 (1948).

33. 321 U.S. 649 (1944).

34. Nixon v. Herndon, 273 U.S. 536 (1924); Nixon v. Condon, 286 U.S. 73 (1932).

35. Grovey v. Townsend, 295 U.S. 45 (1935).

36. Terry v. Adams, 345 U.S. 461 (1953).

37. See Rice v. Elmore, 165 F. 2d 387 (4th Cir. 1948), cert. denied, 333 U.S. 875 (1948).
38. See Berle, "Constitutional Limitations on Corporate Activity—Protection of Personal Rights from Invasion Through Economic Power," 100 *U. Pa. L. Rev.* 933 (1952); Friedmann, "Corporate Power, Government by Private Groups and the Law," 57 *Col. L. Rev.* 155 (1957); St. Antoine, "Color Blindness but Not Myopia: A New Look at State Action, Equal Protection, and 'Private' Racial Discrimination," 59 *Mich. L. Rev.* 993 at 1008 *et. seq.* (1961).
39. See Berle, cited note 38, *supra.*

NOTES TO CHAPTER V

1. Brown v. Board of Education of Topeka, 347 U.S. 483 (1954).
2. See N.Y. *Times,* May 25, 1961, pp. 1 and 24.
3. See N.Y. *Times,* April 27, 1961, p. 1. This effort did not prove successful. See Allen v. County School Board of Prince Edward County (E.D. Va.), 30 *U.S. Law Week* 2018 (1961).
4. 109 U.S. 3 (1883).
5. U.S. Const., Art. I, sec. 2 (House of Representatives); Amendment XVII (Senate).
6. See United States v. Classic, 313 U.S. 299 (1941).
7. U.S. Const., Art. I., sec. 4.
8. 16 Wallace 36 (1873).
9. Crandall v. Nevada, 6 Wallace 35 (1868).
10. See the dissenting opinion in Collins v. Hardyman, 341 U.S. 651 (1951).
11. District of Columbia v. John R. Thompson Co., 346 U.S. 100 (1953).
12. 49 U.S.C.A., secs. 216 (d) and 316 (d).
13. Boynton v. Virginia, 364 U.S. 454 (1960).
14. 18 U.S.C.A., sec. 1074.
15. 29 U.S.C.A., secs. 141 *et seq.*; 18 U.S.C.A., sec. 610.
16. 47 U.S.C.A., sec. 605.
17. 354 U.S. 483 (1954).
18. 29 U.S.C.A., secs. 101-10 and 113-15.
19. See Bush v. Orleans Parish School Board, Williams v. Davis, Governor of Louisiana, 187 F. Supp. 42 (E.D. La. 1960); Bush

v. Orleans Parish School Board, Williams v. Davis, United States v. State of Louisiana, 188 F. Supp. 916 (E.D. La. 1960); Bush v. Orleans Parish School Board, 190 F. Supp. 861, 191 F. Supp. 871 (E.D. La. 1961).

20. See Brewer v. Hoxie School District No. 46 of Lawrence County, Arkansas, 238 F. 2d 91 (8th Cir. 1956), affirming the issuance by the lower court of a decree enjoining private defendants from interfering with the school board's plan for school litigation.

21. Kasper v. Brittain, 245 F. 2d (6th Cir. 1957).

22. See N.Y. *Times*, April 27, 1961, p. 1.

23. The federal district court denied the Attorney General's motion to intervene in the Prince Edward County case. Allen v. County School Board of Prince Edward County, 30 *U.S. Law Week* 2018 (1961).

24. See Bush v. Orleans Parish School Board, 191 F. Supp. 871 (E.D. La. 1961).

25. See Comment, "Constitutional Law—Executive Powers—Use of Troops to Enforce Federal Laws," 56 *Mich. L. Rev.* 249 (1957).

26. Screws v. United States, 325 U.S. 91 (1945).

27. 42 U.S.C.A., sec. 1983.

28. 365 U.S. 167 (1961).

29. See the cases cited in notes 20 and 21, *supra*, involving federal court orders enjoining private persons from interfering with or obstructing the execution by school boards of school desegregation plans.

30. U.S. Const., Art. I, sec. 2; Amendment XVII.

31. United States v. Classic, 313 U.S. 299 (1941).

32. Ex parte Siebold, 100 U.S. 371 (1880).

33. See Ex parte Yarbrough, 110 U.S. 651 (1884); United States v. Classic, 313 U.S. 299 (1941).

34. Breedlove v. Suttles, 302 U.S. 277 (1937).

35. 321 U.S. 649 (1944).

36. 71 Stat. 634, 42 U.S.C.A., secs. 1971, 1975, and 1995; 28 U.S.C.A., secs. 1343 and 1861.

37. 42 U.S.C.A., sec. 1971 (c).

38. United States v. Raines, 362 U.S. 17 (1960).

39. *Ibid.*, p. 27.

40. *Congressional Record*, 85th Cong., 1st Sess., Vol. 103, parts 5-12, *passim*.
41. 42 U.S.C.A., sec. 1995.
42. 42 U.S.C.A., sec. 1975.
43. The Commission's life was extended for another two years. P.L. 86-383, 86th Cong., 1st Sess. (1959).
44. 363 U.S. 420 (1960).
45. 42 U.S.C.A., secs. 1971-74 (e), 1975 (d); 18 U.S.C.A., secs. 837, 1071, and 1509.
46. For the debates, see *Congressional Record*, 86th Cong., 2nd Sess., Vol. 106, parts 4-8, *passim*.
47. 42 U.S.C.A., sec. 1974 (a)-(e).
48. 109 U.S. 3 (1883).
49. U.S. Const., Art. I, sec. 4; Ex parte Siebold, 100 U.S. 371 (1880).
50. Ex parte Yarbrough, 110 U.S. 651 (1884).
51. 42 U.S.C.A., sec. 1971.
52. In a proceeding brought by the United States under the Civil Rights Act of 1957, 42 U.S.C.A., sec. 1971 (c), the Court of Appeals for the Sixth Circuit has held that the government was entitled to a preliminary injunction restraining the defendant white landowners from engaging in any threats against Negro tenants, whether by eviction, threatened eviction, or refusal to deal with them in good faith, for the purpose of interfering with their right to register and to vote for candidates for federal office. United States v. Beaty, United States v. Barcroft, 288 F. 2d 653 (6th Cir. 1961).
53. See Kasper v. Brittain, 245 F. 2d 92 (6th Cir. 1957), upholding a contempt order against a private person for obstructing enforcement of a desegregation decree.
54. Brewer v. Hoxie School District No. 46 of Lawrence County, Arkansas, 238 F. 2d 91 (8th Cir. 1956). See note 20, *supra*.
55. See the references to the Prince Edward County case in notes 3, 22, and 23, *supra*, and the discussion in the text at those points.
56. 10 U.S.C.A., sec. 333.
57. For various phases of the Montgomery situation, see N.Y. *Times*, May 21, 1961, p. 1; May 22, p. 26; May 23, p. 26; May 24, pp. 1 and 24; May 26, pp. 20 and 24; June 3, pp. 1 and 18.

58. See *In re* Debs, 158 U.S. 564 (1895).
59. Sec. 333, 10 U.S.C.A., does not actually limit the President to the use of militia or the armed forces. It authorizes the use also of "any other means." Federal marshals and other federal law-enforcement agents would come under "any other means." Presumably the President could delegate to the Attorney General his authority to call out marshals or other agents for the purpose of this section.
60. When the President calls out the militia or the armed forces under authority of Sec. 333, he is required by Sec. 334, by proclamation, "to immediately order the insurgents to disperse and retire peaceably to their abodes within a limited time." Whether this requirement implicitly applies when "other means" are employed under Sec. 333 is not clear. No proclamation was issued by President Kennedy in connection with the Montgomery crisis.
61. 28 U.S.C.A., secs. 547 and 549.

TABLE OF CASES

Adamson v. California, 211 n. 3
Alberts v. California, 66, 68, 71, 82, 88, 114, 212 n. 23 & n. 28
Allen v. County School Board of Prince Edward County, 220 n. 3, 221 n. 23
American Communications Assn., C.I.O. v. Douds, 107, 215 n. 11
American Federation v. Swing, 218 n. 15
Anastaplo, In re, 216 n. 24 & n. 36
Anderson v. Swart, 210 n. 46
Bantam Books, Inc. v. Melko, 213 n. 34
Barenblatt v. United States, 95, 121, 212 n. 16, 216 n. 35 & n. 37
Bates v. City of Little Rock, 101
Beauharnais v. Illinois, 58, 211 n. 4
Beilan v. Board of Education, 215 n. 10
Black v. Cutter Laboratories, 149
Boynton v. Virginia, 156, 178
Braden v. United States, 216 n. 23
Bradfield v. Roberts, 208 n. 28
Braunfeld v. Brown, 207 n. 5, 208 n. 17, 217 n. 44
Breard v. City of Alexandria, Louisiana, 211 n. 10
Breedlove v. Suttles, 221 n. 34
Brewer v. Hoxie School District

No. 46 of Lawrence County, Arkansas, 221 n. 20, 222 n. 54
Bridges v. California, 211 n. 7
Brown v. Board of Education, 167, 182
Burton v. Wilmington Park Authority, 144, 158, 219 n. 21 & n. 28
Bush v. Orleans Parish School Board, 220 n. 19, 221 n. 24
Butler v. Michigan, 66
Buxton v. Ullman, 208 n. 22 & n. 23
Cantwell v. Connecticut, 207 n. 8
Chaplinsky v. New Hampshire, 212 n. 15
Civil Rights Cases, 132, 140, 157, 166, 172, 200
Cochran v. Louisiana Board of Education, 210 n. 42
Collins v. Hardyman, 220 n. 10
Commercial Pictures Corp. v. Regents of University of State of New York, 213 n. 39
Commonwealth v. Gordon, 212 n. 27
Commonwealth v. Isenstadt, 212 n. 26
Communist Party of the United States v. Subversive Activities Control Board, 90, 216 n. 22 & n. 28, 217 n. 49
Craig v. Harney, 211 n. 7
Crandall v. Nevada, 177

Debs, In re, 223 n. 58
Dennis v. United States, 93, 109, 125, 211 n. 5, 216 n. 25 & n. 33, 217 n. 38
Derrington v. Plummer, 219 n. 29
District of Columbia v. John R. Thompson Co., 220 n. 11
Doe v. Ullman, 208 n. 22 & n. 23
Doremus v. Board of Education, 208 n. 24, 209 n. 30
Dorsey v. Stuyvesant Town Corporation, 219 n. 25
Eaton v. Price, 211 n. 4
Engel v. Vitale, 209 n. 29
Everson v. Board of Education, 11, 13, 22, 24, 35, 43, 46, 207 n. 6, n. 7, n. 9, & n. 11, 209 n. 39
Frothingham v. Mellon, 34
Gallagher v. Crown Kosher Super Market of Massachusetts, Inc., 207 n. 5, 208 n. 17, 217 n. 44
Garner v. Board of Public Works, 215 n. 10 & n. 11
Gelling v. Texas, 78
Giboney v. Empire Storage and Ice Company, 211 n. 13
Girard College Trusteeship, In re, 218 n. 7
Gitlow v. New York, 216 n. 34
Grosjean v. American Press Company, 211 n. 6
Grovey v. Townsend, 219 n. 35
Hall v. Commonwealth of Virginia, 219 n. 32
Hannah v. Larche, 198
Harisiades v. Shaughnessy, 217 n. 38
Hill v. Texas, 218 n. 5

H.M.H. Publishing Co. v. Garrett, 213 n. 34
Holmby Productions, Inc. v. Vaughn, 213 n. 40
Hughes v. Superior Court of California, 212 n. 13
International Association of Machinists v. Street, 215 n. 19, 216 n. 20
Joseph Burstyn, Inc. v. Wilson, 76, 77
Kasper v. Brittain, 221 n. 21, 222 n. 53
Kerr v. Enoch Pratt Free Public Library, 219 n. 30
Kingsley Books, Inc. v. Brown, 213 n. 32, 214 n. 48
Kingsley International Pictures Corp. v. Regents of the University of the State of New York, 70, 79
Konigsberg v. State Bar of California (353 U.S. 252), 215 n. 8
Konigsberg v. State Bar of California (366 U.S. 36), 95, 211 n. 5, 212 n. 16, 216 n. 24, n. 36, & n. 37, 217 n. 39
Kunz v. New York, 207 n. 8, 208 n. 26
Lathrop v. Donohue, 215 n. 19, 216 n. 21
Lawrence v. Hancock, 219 n. 26
Louisiana v. NAACP, 96
Lovell v. City of Griffin, 56, 83
Marcus v. Search Warrant of Property at 104 East Tenth Street, Kansas City, Missouri, 213 n. 34, 214 n. 47a
Marsh v. Alabama, 160, 219 n. 32
Martin v. City of Struthers, 211 n. 11

McCollum v. Board of Education, 14, 15, 23, 25

McCulloch v. Maryland, 131

McGowan v. Maryland, 24, 25, 207 n. 5, 208 n. 17 & n. 18

Monroe v. Pape, 140, 189, 218 n. 10

Murdock v. Pennsylvania, 207 n. 8

Mutual Film Corporation v. Industrial Commission, 75, 76

NAACP v. Alabama, 100

National Labor Relations Board v. Jones and Laughlin Steel Corporation, 215 n. 17

Near v. Minnesota, 54, 55, 62, 82, 212 n. 18

New American Library of World Literature, Inc. v. Allen, 213 n. 34

Niemotko v. Maryland, 208 n. 26

Nixon v. Condon, 219 n. 34

Nixon v. Herndon, 219 n. 34

Norris v. Alabama, 218 n. 5

Norris v. Mayor & City Council of Baltimore, 219 n. 30

Patton v. Mississippi, 218 n. 5

Pennekamp v. Florida, 211 n. 7

Pennsylvania v. Board of Directors of City Trusts of the City of Philadelphia (350 U.S. 230), 138

Pennsylvania v. Board of Directors of City Trusts of the City of Philadelphia (357 U.S. 570), 218 n. 7

People of New York ex rel. Bryant v. Zimmerman, 215 n. 13

People v. Richmond County News, Inc., 212 n. 29

Pierce v. Society of Sisters, 24, 45

Poe v. Ullman, 208 n. 22 & n. 23, 211 n. 3

Prince v. Massachusetts, 217 n. 43

Regina v. Hicklin, 67, 68, 69

Reynolds v. United States, 217 n. 42

Rice v. Elmore, 220 n. 37

Rice v. Sioux City Memorial Park Cemetery (245 Iowa 147), 218 n. 18

Rice v. Sioux City Memorial Park Cemetery (348 U.S. 880), 148, 219 n. 19

Rice v. Sioux City Memorial Park Cemetery (349 U.S. 70), 219 n. 19

Roth v. United States, 66, 68, 71, 82, 88, 114, 211 n. 4, 212 n. 23 & n. 28

Scales v. United States, 93, 122, 125, 211 n. 5, 216 n. 26, n. 32, n. 33, & n. 37

Schemp v. School District of Abington Township, 208 n. 29

Schneider v. Town of Irvington, 211 n. 9

School District of Abington Township v. Schemp, 209 n. 29

Screws v. United States, 140, 141, 188

Shelley v. Kraemer, 146, 148, 150, 164, 218 n. 17

Shelton v. Tucker, 101, 215 n. 12

Siebold, Ex parte, 221 n. 32

Slaughter-House Cases, 176

Smith v. Allwright, 160, 164, 196

Smith v. California, 211 n. 4, 213 n. 33

Southern Pacific Co. v. Arizona, 118

Speiser v. Randall, 210 n. 2

Steward Machine Co. v. Davis, 209 n. 38

Superior Films, Inc. v. Dept. of Education of Ohio, Division of Censorship, 213 n. 38

Swart v. Smith Burlington Town School District, 210 n. 46

Tate v. Department of Conservation and Development, 219 n. 27

Terry v. Adams, 219 n. 36

Thornhill v. Alabama, 211 n. 12

Times Film Corporation v. City of Chicago (355 U.S. 35), 213 n. 41

Times Film Corporation v. City of Chicago (365 U.S. 43), 85, 214 n. 45

Torcaso v. Watkins, 207 n. 4 & n. 12

Two Guys from Harrison-Allentown, Inc. v. McGinley, 207 n. 5, 208 n. 17

United States v. Barcroft, 222 n. 52

United States v. Beaty, 222 n. 52

United States v. Butler, 209 n. 38

United States v. Causby, 217 n. 48

United States v. C.I.O., 215 n. 18

United States v. Classic, 141, 220 n. 6, 221 n. 31 & n. 33

United States v. Harriss, 215 n. 18

United States v. International Union United Automobile, etc., Workers of America, 215 n. 18

United States v. Kennerley, 212 n. 25

United States v. One Book Called "Ulysses," 212 n. 25

United States v. Oregon, 217 n. 45

United States v. Raines, 197, 221 n. 39

United States v. State of Louisiana, 221 n. 19

Village of Euclid v. Ambler Realty Company, 217 n. 47

Virginia, Ex parte, 141, 218 n. 13

Watchtower Bible, etc. Society v. Metropolitan Life Insurance Company, 219 n. 32

West Virginia State Board of Education v. Barnette, 207 n. 8

Whitney v. California, 216 n. 34

Wilkinson v. United States, 95, 216 n. 23 & n. 35

Williams v. Davis, Governor of Louisiana, 220 n. 19

Winters v. New York, 66, 78

Yarbrough, Ex parte, 221 n. 33, 222 n. 50

Yates v. United States, 93, 109, 122, 216 n. 25 & n. 31

Yick Wo v. Hopkins, 138

Zorach v. Clauson, 15, 18, 25, 207 n. 9, 208 n. 16, 209 n. 31

INDEX

Absolutist interpretation of First Amendment, 111-25. *See also* Balancing of interests; First Amendment; Speech, freedom of

Aid to religion. *See also* Church-State; Establishment of religion
Bible-reading in public schools, 39-41
bus transportation, 11, 46
chaplains, military, 35-36
church colleges, 48-49
concurrence of function, 37-39, 47
federal aid to parochial schools, 42-48
free lunches for school children, 46
hospitals, church operated, 38-39
loans to parochial schools, 48
National Defense Educational Act, 47
preserving the peace, 27
religious education in public schools, 39-41
tax exemptions, 36
textbooks, school, 46
use of public property, 37
Antilynch laws, 190-92
Association, freedom of. *See also* Balancing of interests; Communist Party; Disclosure of membership, freedom from; Due process clause; First Amendment; N.A.A.C.P.; Smith Act; Speech, freedom of
business ventures, 103
Communist Party, 106-10
disclosure of membership, 92, 101
due process freedom, 101
First Amendment, 97, 106
fundamental right, 97, 102-4
generally, 90-110
labor unions and trade associations, 102-3
N.A.A.C.P., 96-98, 100-101, 106-10
nonpolitical, nonprofit groups, 99-100, 102
political parties, 99
substantive freedom, 100-101
Attorney General of United States
desegregation enforcement, 202-5
federal marshals, 203
Prince Edward County, Virginia, 185-86
voting rights enforcement, 197

Balancing of interests. *See also* Association, freedom of; Communist Party; Disclosure of membership, freedom from; First Amendment; Speech, freedom of

Balancing of interests (*Cont.*)
freedom of press, 59-60
judicial technique in interpretation of First Amendment, 111-25
Bar, admission to
freedom of nonassociation, 105
membership disclosure as condition, 95-96
Bible-reading, 39-41
Birth control laws, 30-33
Black, Justice Hugo, 11, 13, 79-80, 84, 88, 111-14
Booksellers, 71
Bus transportation, 11, 46

Catholic Church
birth control, 30-33
church-state position, 3
federal aid to schools, 43
Censorship. *See also* Movies; Obscenity laws; Press, freedom of; Prior restraint
enjoining sale of book, 70-71
movies, 74-89
press, freedom of, 60-63
Chaplains, military, 35-36
Church colleges, 48-49
Church-State. *See also* Aid to religion; Establishment of religion; Religious freedom; Separation of church and state
aid to religion prohibited, 13-14, 33-34
concurrence of function, 37-39, 47
generally, 3-51
judicial interpretation, 11-25
Civil liberties. *See also* Civil Rights Acts; Congressional power; Due process; Equal

protection; Racial discrimination; Voting rights
Congressional role, 187-202, 205-6
definition, 169-70
executive role, 181, 202-5
federal government's role, 167-206
judicial role, 168, 183-87
protected versus created rights, 171-81
voting rights, 182
Civil rights
civil liberties contrasted, 130
definition, 170
nature and basis of, 129-30
Civil Rights Act, 187, 192
Civil Rights Act of 1957, 201-2, 206
Civil Rights Act of 1960, 199, 202, 206
Civil Rights Commission, 198-99
Civil War, 188
Clark, Justice Thomas C., 82, 85
Clear and present danger. *See also* Association, freedom of; Balancing of interests; Speech, freedom of
freedom of press, 56
test of obscenity, 68
Colleges and universities
federal aid to, 48-49
religious instruction, 41-42
Communist Party. *See also* Association, freedom of; Congressional power; Disclosure of membership, freedom from; Internal Security Act; Smith Act; Speech, freedom of
advocacy of forcible overthrow, 93

Communist Party (*Cont.*)
Congressional investigation, 108-
  10, 121
contrasted with N.A.A.C.P., 97-
  98, 106-10
disclosure of membership, 107,
  113
Internal Security Act, 106
knowing membership under
  Smith Act, 93-94
methods of control, 125-26
registration of, 90-93
Smith Act, 107
status as political party, 90-98,
  107
Compulsory school laws, 44
Concurrence of function
education, 47
secular and religious, 37-39
Congressional legislation
civil liberties, 187-202, 205-6
criminal laws, 188
remedial measures, 188-90
voting rights, 192-202
Congressional powers
antilynch legislation, 190-92
District of Columbia, 177-78
enforcement of Fourteenth
  Amendment, 133
interstate commerce, 178-79
investigative power, 95, 108-10,
  121. *See also* Communist
  Party; Disclosure of membership, freedom from; First
  Amendment; Speech, freedom
  of
poll tax legislation, 194-95
spending power, 179
Constitutional rights, 130
Contempt orders, 56
Created rights, 174-80

Criminal Code, U.S., 188, 192,
  202

Desegregation of schools
equal protection, 182-83
equity power of federal courts,
  183-87
federal government's power,
  167-68
Prince Edward County, Virginia,
  168
Disclosure of membership, freedom from. *See also* Association, freedom of; Communist
  Party; First Amendment;
  N.A.A.C.P.; Speech, freedom
  of
admission to bar, 96
balancing of interests, 101, 110
Communist Party, 106-10, 113
Congressional investigations, 95-
  96, 110.
due process, 96, 101
First Amendment, 95-96, 110
generally, 90-110
Ku Klux Klan, 98
N.A.A.C.P., 98, 106-10
Discrimination. *See* Civil liberties;
  Equal protection; Racial dis-
  crimination; Voting rights
Distribution of literature, 56-57
District of Columbia, 177-78
Douglas, Justice William, 15, 17-
  25, 78-80, 84, 111-12
Due process clause. *See also*
  Balancing of interests; Estab-
  lishment of religion; First
  Amendment; Fourteenth
  Amendment; Fundamental
  rights; Political association,
  freedom of; Religious freedom;

Speech, freedom of; State action
applicability to state action in all forms, 136-55
association, freedom of, 101
birth control laws, 32
disclosure, freedom from, 101
movie censorship, 85-86
press, freedom of, 53-55, 57-59, 85-86

Eisenhower, President Dwight D., 186, 203
Equal protection. *See also* Civil liberties; Racial discrimination; Restrictive covenants; State action; Voting rights
enforcement of trespass statute, 153-55
interpretation, 128-29
judicial enforcement of restrictive covenants, 146-49
judicial interpretation of private rights, 142-43
lease of public property, 158-59
private discrimination, 184
racial discrimination, 143-45, 154-55
real estate dealers, 163
school desegregation, 182-83
state action, 134-35
state inaction, 127-28, 139
statutory discrimination, 144-45
voting rights, 182, 193, 200
Establishment of religion. *See also* Aid to religion; Church-State; Separation of church and state
aid to religion prohibited, 13-14, 33-34
concurrence of function, 37-39, 47

Establishment of religion (*Cont.*)
general considerations, 9-39
judicial interpretation, 11-25
released time for religious instruction, 14-19
religion in public schools, 14-19, 39-41
Sunday closing laws, 19-25
tax exemptions, 36

Federal Communications Act, 179
Federal courts, 167-68, 183-87
Federal government. *See also* Aid to religion; Church-State; Civil liberties; Congressional powers; Equal protection; Establishment of religion; Voting rights
aid to education, 5, 14, 42-48
obscenity legislation, 72-73
role respecting civil liberties, 167-206
Fifteenth Amendment
Negro voting rights, 182
primary elections, 161
voting rights, 129, 195-96
First Amendment. *See also* Aid to religion; Balancing of interests; Church-State; Communist Party; Disclosure of membership, freedom from; Due process clause; Establishment of religion; Fourteenth Amendment; Internal Security Act; Obscenity laws; Press, freedom of; Smith Act; Speech, freedom of
absolutist interpretation, 111-25
advocacy of forcible overthrow, 121-23
as limitation on states, 7-8, 73

First Amendment (*Cont.*)
balancing of interests, 59-60, 94-95, 111-25
categories of protected freedoms, 119-20
incorporation into Fourteenth Amendment, 7-8, 73
Internal Security Act of 1950, 120
judicial techniques in interpretation, 111-25
preferred freedoms, 86, 111-14, 119
Fourteenth Amendment. *See also* Aid to religion; Civil liberties; Due process clause; Equal protection; Establishment of religion; First Amendment; Fundamental rights; Press, freedom of; Racial discrimination; Speech, freedom of; State action
civil rights legislation, 132
color of law, 140-41, 191
Congressional enforcement power, 131-34, 172-74
freedom from disclosure, 96
freedom of association, 97
incorporation of First Amendment, 7-8, 54-55, 73
judicial role, 173-74
private persons as state agents, 155-66
privileges and immunities clause, 176-77
protected rights, 172-74
restraint on state agencies, 127-66
state inaction, 138-39
United States as party in interest, 186

Franchised businesses as state agencies, 156-57
Frankfurter, Justice Felix, 22-25, 35, 77, 112
Freedom Riders, 168, 178-79
Free lunch program, 46
Fundamental rights. *See also* Association, freedom of; Church-State; Due process clause; Establishment of religion; Fourteenth Amendment; Press, freedom of; Speech, freedom of
freedom of press, 53-55, 57
free exercise of religion, 8-9

General welfare spending, 43-44. *See also* Federal government
Girard Trust, 138
Grant, President Ulysses S., 31

Harlan, Justice John M. (1877-1911), 132
Harlan, Justice John M., 32, 112, 114
Higher education, federal aid, 5, 48
Hill-Burton Act, 39
Holmes, Justice Oliver Wendell, Jr., 86, 112
Holmes-Brandeis test, 110
Hospitals, aid to church-operated, 38-39
Hotels and innkeepers, 143-45
Hughes, Chief Justice Charles E., 63

Immoral as test of obscenity, 70
Incorporation of First Amendment into Fourteenth, 7-8, 54-55, 73

Injunction against sale of books, 70-71

Internal Security Act, 90-91, 106, 108, 125

Interstate Commerce Act, 156-57

Jaybird Party, 161

Jefferson, Thomas, 11-12

Jehovah's Witnesses, 37, 135, 160

Judicial enforcement of private right, 142-53

Judicial review. *See also* Balancing of interests; First Amendment
examination of films, 88-89
interpretation of First Amendment, 111-26

Justice Department, 181, 183, 202, 205

Kennedy, President John F., 3, 43, 48, 203

Ku Klux Klan, 98, 168, 188, 203

Labor unions
freedom of association, 103
freedom of nonassociation, 105

Lady Chatterley's Lover, 79

Libel laws, 58-59

List circulation, 72

Little Rock, Arkansas, 187

Loans to parochial schools, 48

Marshall, Chief Justice John, 131

Miracle, The, 76

Montgomery, Alabama, 168-203

Movies. *See also* Censorship; Due process clause; Fourteenth Amendment; Obscenity laws; Press, freedom of; Prior restraint

Movies (*Cont.*)
censorship of, 74-89
review by court, 88-89

N.A.A.C.P., 96-101, 106-10, 186. *See also* Association, freedom of; Disclosure of membership, freedom from

National Defense Educational Act of 1958, 47

National Labor Relations Act, 107, 179

Negroes. *See* Civil liberties; Equal protection; Racial discrimination; Sit-in demonstrations; State action; Trespass statutes; Voting rights

New Orleans, La., 184

Nonassociation, freedom of
balancing of interests, 105
bar membership, 105
labor union membership, 105

Norris-LaGuardia Act, 183

Obscenity laws. *See also* Censorship; Due process clause; Movies; Press, freedom of
as vague and indefinite, 64
booksellers, enforcement against, 71
clear and present danger, 68
constitutionality, 64-74
definition of obscene, 68-69
enforcement and remedial problems, 65
enjoining sale of books, 70-71
Federal government, 72-73
free press, 64-74
generally, 52-89
immoral ideas, 70
movie censorship, 81-84

Parochial schools. *See also* Aid to
    religion; Church-State; Estab-
    lishment of religion; Federal
    government
  bus transportation, 11-14, 46
  federal aid to, 42-48
  financial aid to, 5, 42-48
  freedom to operate, 45
  free lunches, 40
  general welfare, 44
  loans to, 48
  National Defense Educational
    Act, 47
  parents' freedom to choose, 45
  textbooks, 46
Picketing, 57
Police power. *See also* Movies;
    Obscenity laws
  protect morals, 52
  restriction on religious freedom,
    21
Political parties, 99
Poll tax legislation, 194-95
Preferred freedoms of First
    Amendment, 55, 86
Press, freedom of. *See also* Cen-
    sorship; Due process clause;
    First Amendment; Movies;
    Obscenity laws; Prior restraint
  basic principles, 57-63
  censorship, 60-63
  clear and present danger, 56
  contempt orders, 56
  distribution of literature, 56-57
  due process clause, 58-59, 85-86
  fundamental right, 57
  generally, 52-89
  libel laws, 58-59, 114-15
  movies, 75-76
  obscenity laws, 64-74
  picketing, 57

Press (*Cont.*)
  post restraints, 60-63
  prior restraints, 60-63
  tax on newspapers, 56
Primary elections, 160-61. *See
    also* Equal protection; Racial
    discrimination; Voting rights
Prince Edward County, Virginia,
    168, 185-86
Prior restraint. *See also* Censor-
    ship; Movies; Obscenity laws;
    Press, freedom of
  censorship of movies, 74-89
  circulation of book lists, 72
  enjoining sale of books, 70-71
  freedom of press, 60-63, 84-87
Private discrimination. *See* Equal
    protection; Racial discrimina-
    tion; State action
Private rights, 142-55
Privileges and immunities, 176-77
Protected rights, 171-74
Protestant influence, 4
Public employment, 110
Public property, religious use of,
    37
Public schools. *See also* Aid to re-
    ligion; Church-State; Estab-
    lishment of religion; Religious
    education
  Bible-reading, 39-41
  released time, 39-40
  religious education, 39-41
Racial discrimination. *See also*
    Civil liberties; Equal protec-
    tion; State action
  hotels and innkeepers, 143-44
  leasing of public property, 158-
    59
  real estate dealers, 163
  restaurants, 144-45

Racial discrimination (*Cont.*)
  restrictive covenants, 146-49
  sit-in demonstrations, 134-35,
    153-55
  trespass statutes, 134-35, 153-55
Reed, Justice Stanley, 14, 77
Religious education. *See also* Aid
    to religion; Colleges and uni-
    versities; Establishment of re-
    ligion; Parochial schools;
    Public schools
  colleges and universities, 41-42
  federal aid to parochial schools,
    42-48
  public schools, 39-41
  released time, 14-19
  state constitutions, 42
Religious freedom. *See also*
    Church-State; Establishment
    of religion
  dependence on separation, 9-10
  freedom from discrimination, 37
  limitations on, 114-15
  scope of, 9
  Sunday closing laws, 19-25
Restaurants and innkeepers, 143-
    45, 153-55
Restrictive covenants, 146-49. *See
    also* Equal Protection; State
    action
Rights under Constitution
  created rights, 174-80
  protected rights, 171-74

Self-incrimination. *See* Com-
    munist Party
Separation of church and state.
    See also Aid to religion;
    Church-State; Establishment
    of religion; Religious freedom
  general critique, 26-33

Separation of church and state
    (*Cont.*)
  interdependence, 27-31
  separateness of functions, 27-31
  symbolic language, 6
Sit-in demonstrations, 134-35,
    153-55
Smith Act, 91-94, 107-8, 113,
    121-25. *See also* Association,
    freedom of; Balancing of in-
    terests; Communist Party;
    First Amendment; Speech,
    freedom of
Speech, freedom of. *See also* Asso-
    ciation, freedom of; Balancing
    of interests; Communist Party;
    Congressional investigations;
    Due process clause; First
    Amendment; Fourteenth
    Amendment; Fundamental
    rights
  activities included, 114-15
  business and labor organizations,
    103
  clear and present danger, 110,
    122
  criticism of government, 108-9
  Holmesian-Brandeis test, 110
  judicial techniques, 111-25
  political activities, 119-20
Standing to question federal
    spending, 33-35
State action. *See also* Due process
    clause; Equal protection;
    Racial discrimination; Voting
    rights
  carriers, 156-57
  color of law, 140-41
  corporations, 163-65
  generally, 127-65

State action (*Cont.*)
  instrumentality theory, 155
  judicial acts, 141-55
  judicial enforcement of private
    rights, 142-53
  lawless acts of officials, 139-41
  legislative enactments, 136-37
  lessees of state property, 157-59
  licensed activities, 162-63
  performance of state functions,
    160-61
  primary elections, 160-61
  private employers, 150
  privileged private persons, 155-
    66
  property administration, 138
  publicly assisted functions, 159
  public utilities, 156-57
  regulated businesses, 161-62
  restrictive covenants, 149
State constitutions, 7, 42
Stewart, Justice Potter, 80, 144
Subversive Activities Control
    Board, 90, 93, 107, 121
Sunday closing laws, 19-25, 37

Tax exemptions, 36

Tax funds. *See* Aid to religion;
    Establishment of religion;
    Parochial schools; Religious
    education
Tax on newspapers, 56
Taxpayer's standing to question
    spending, 34-35
Trespass statute enforcement, 134-
    35, 153-55

Vague and indefinite statute, 64
Voting rights. *See also* Equal pro-
    tection; Racial discrimination;
    State action
  Congressional legislation, 176,
    193-94, 200-202
  federal elections, 192-95
  federally created rights, 175-76
  federal supervision, 199
  judicial enforcement, 197
  poll taxes, 194-95
  primary elections, 161
  private coercion, 199-200
  racial discrimination, 192-202
  state and local elections, 192-97

Warren, Chief Justice Earl, 22,
    83-84